Conceptualizing Reflection in Teacher Development

Conceptualizing Reflection in Teacher Development

Edited by

James Calderhead and Peter Gates

 The Falmer Press

(A Member of the Taylor & Francis Group)
London • Washington, D.C.

UK   The Falmer Press, 4 John St, London WC1N 2ET
USA The Falmer Press, Taylor & Francis Inc., 1900 Frost Road, Suite 101,
         Bristol PA 19007

First published 1993

A catalogue record for this book is available from the British Library

ISBN 0 75070 123 4 cased
ISBN 0 75070 124 2 paperback

**Library of Congress Cataloging-in-Publication Data are available on
request**

Jacket design by Caroline Archer

Typeset in 10/12pt Times by
Graphicraft Typesetters Ltd., Hong Kong

*Printed in Great Britain by Burgess Science Press, Basingstoke on
paper which has a specified pH value on final paper manufacture of
not less than 7.5 and is therefore 'acid free'.*

Contents

Contents

Introduction

James Calderhead and Peter Gates

Reflection has come to be widely recognized as a crucial element in the professional growth of teachers. Terms such as 'reflective teaching', 'inquiry-oriented teacher education', 'teacher as researcher' and 'reflective practitioner' have become quite prolific in discussions of classroom practice and professional development. It is frequently presumed that reflection is an intrinsically good and desirable aspect of teaching and teacher education, and that teachers, in becoming more reflective, will in some sense be better teachers, though such claims have rarely been subjected to detailed scrutiny.

Reflective terminology, however, is being used in various ways, and is informed by diverse theoretical frameworks. The work of John Dewey (1933) has been particularly influential. His distinction between action based on reflection and action that is impulsive or blind, and his emphasis on the need to develop certain attitudes of open-mindedness and skills of thinking and reasoning in order to reflect have shaped the way that many researchers and teacher educators have thought about reflective teaching. Donald Schön (1983) has also been influential with the notion of reflection-in-action — the idea that professionals engage in reflective conversations with practical situations, where they constantly frame and reframe a problem as they work on it, testing out their interpretations and solutions. Experiential learning and work in adult learning, drawing upon the work of Kolb (1984) for example, has had some influence. Critical theory, including the work of Carr and Kemmis (1986), has stimulated considerable thought about the importance of increasing teachers' awareness of the causes and consequences of their action through research on their own situation.

The current enthusiasm for reflective teaching may be partly explained in terms of an attempt to understand more fully what is distinctive about teachers' professional development and to come to terms with its complexity. It might also be partly explained in terms of a reaction against current trends in many Western countries towards an increasing centralization in the control of education. At a time when teachers are increasingly being portrayed in educational policy as technicians or deliverers of the curriculum, reflective teaching offers promise of an alternative conceptualization that appropriately recognizes the thoughtful and professional aspects of teachers' work. With education in some countries becoming highly politicized, reflective teaching has also been associated with a call for teacher empowerment and emancipation, enabling teachers to examine ideologies critically and to consider the value basis of their own practice.

What reflective teaching amounts to, what its contribution is to the professional development of teachers today and whether its promises are in fact being fulfilled have become important questions that have recently attracted several conceptual analyses, empirical research studies and evaluation projects. The purpose of this book is to draw together a selection of this work, to examine the nature of reflection in teachers' professional development and to consider its contribution to the ongoing development of teachers.

Issues in Reflective Teaching

Teacher education programmes based on notions of reflective practice frequently espouse one or more of the following aims:

- to enable teachers to analyze, discuss, evaluate and change their own practice, adopting an analytical approach towards teaching;
- to foster teachers' appreciation of the social and political contexts in which they work, helping teachers to recognize that teaching is socially and politically situated and that the teacher's task involves an appreciation and analysis of that context;
- to enable teachers to appraise the moral and ethical issues implicit in classroom practices, including the critical examination of their own beliefs about good teaching;
- to encourage teachers to take greater responsibility for their own professional growth and to acquire some degree of professional autonomy;
- to facilitate teachers' development of their own theories of educational practice, understanding and developing a principled basis for their own classroom work;
- to empower teachers so that they may better influence future directions in education and take a more active role in educational decision-making.

In implementing these aims, a variety of reflective tools have been employed — action research, reflective journals, the use of theory and research evidence to interpret practice, coaching, etc.

Despite the proliferation of diverse reflective teaching methods and programs, one feature about which there is a great deal of agreement is the difficulty of putting ideas about reflective teaching into practice. This in turn has led to the identification of a number of issues in conceptualizing and promoting teacher reflection, as outlined below, which frequently express themselves as dilemmas for the teacher educator (see Calderhead, 1992).

1)   What is the process of growth in developing reflection?
Much has been written on the importance of developing reflection in teachers, and as teacher educators we frequently criticize student teachers for not being able to reflect upon, evaluate and analyze their own practice. But what is it that the student teacher lacks? — skills, attitudes or dispositions? And if we are referring to skills, are these very high level skills — in which case, what are the processes of development in achieving these skills? Do student teachers, for example, go through a phase of developing taken-for-granted routines before they are in a position to analyze and critically evaluate them? Are we by emphasizing reflection with student teachers aiming too high? And what do we do to prepare students for reflection?

2)   What is the relationship between 'personal' knowledge and 'public' knowledge?
In encouraging teachers to analyze and evaluate their practice, the teaching context and the beliefs and values that are implicit within it, student teachers are being encouraged to develop their own knowledge through an examination of practice, but what is the relationship of this to the body of knowledge within the teacher education curriculum? In what ways can we attempt to integrate the knowledge that grows from reflection on practice with other knowledge, such as theoretical knowledge and empirical research evidence, that we deem to be of value in teacher education?

3)   How do we accommodate professional growth and emancipation?
Metaphors of professional growth and development seem to suggest a continuum of predefined experience, but programs of reflective practice are also frequently attempting to ensure that teachers take responsibility for their own professional development, which necessarily requires the objectives of the training to be much more open-ended and negotiable. Should a truly reflective teaching program have predefined content or should it be negotiated? How does one reconcile the aim of developing particular areas of knowledge, skill and attitudes with the aim of encouraging autonomy and professional responsibility?

4)   How do we accommodate reflective practice in schools?
While reflective teaching programs can embody a variety of particular values, especially about teaching and about professional development, these are frequently in conflict with the values that are traditionally held

in schools. The notion that teachers require time to analyze what they are doing and consider the educational worth of their practices, for example, is often at odds with the priorities in schools which typically attach a much higher value to immediate, unreflective action. Student teachers clearly experience these conflicts and teacher educators face various dilemmas in how they present their programs to satisfy their aims but also maintain credibility in the eyes of student and experienced teachers.

5) How do we reconcile concerns with assessment with concerns for reflection?

Traditionally in teacher education, teacher educators have served a gatekeeping function, guarding entry and ensuring quality control in the production of teachers. It has generally been regarded as an important function of their work to assess their students and to ensure that only the committed and the competent gain entry to the profession. This assessment role, however, is somewhat at odds with the role of facilitator frequently demanded in reflective teaching programs, where the criteria of effectiveness are not so much concerned with competence at a behavioral level as much as competence at the level of awareness and critical appraisal. Furthermore, the role of assessor may also impede the role of facilitator. If student teachers know they are to be assessed by their tutors or supervizing teachers, they may be much more reluctant to confide in them and discuss their concerns and difficulties openly.

6) How do we cater for individual differences in learning to teach?

We know that student teachers learn to teach in various ways, approaching the task with quite different background experiences. Some are well oriented to learn in a reflective teaching program, others are not (Korthagen, 1988). Students also come to preservice training with various entrenched ideas and beliefs about teaching, learning and the curriculum, as a result of their childhood experiences in school, which predispose them to consider classroom practice in particular ways (Calderhead and Robson, 1988). How do we take account of these differences in a reflective teacher education program?

7) What can be reasonably expected of student teachers during the course of a preservice program and what is only feasible in the much longer term, after considerable experience in the classroom and further inservice support?

The aims of preservice reflective teaching programs are quite often highly ambitious and set targets that are probably impossible to achieve with the majority of students in the time available. Becoming a teacher who is aware of their own values and beliefs, able to analyze their own practice and consider its ethical basis and its social and political context

involves considerable ability and experience, and may well be beyond
the capabilities of most student teachers in the time span of a preservice
program. Deciding what is reasonable for student teachers to achieve
in such a program and what can more realistically be achieved in
subsequent inservice training, and deciding on how continuity of training might be ensured, are tasks teacher educators currently have to
consider.

8) What consideration do we have to give to the teaching context?
In designing preservice training programs it is fairly common practice to
think of the program as relatively self-contained. But research indicates
that the ethos of the schools in which students eventually teach are also
a major influence. If reflective teaching programs are to affect the working lives of teachers, teacher educators must bear in mind not just the
immediate integrity of the program but how it copes with the other
demands that will be placed upon student teachers' practice, and in
particular how it might be responsive to the contexts in which they will
find themselves as teachers.

9) To what extent is reflection an individual or collective pursuit?
Discussions of reflective teaching frequently dwell upon the individual
teacher, and the individual capacity to analyze and evaluate practice and
the context in which it occurs. But there is some evidence to suggest that
reflective practice requires a supportive environment in which it can be
fostered (e.g. Zeichner and Liston, 1987). It may only be within a culture of collaboration that beginning teachers are encouraged to develop
as reflective practitioners. This raises the question of whether reflective teaching may be a more appropriate aim to consider in relation
to schools or groups of teachers rather than in relation to individual
teachers. And it raises questions about where teacher educators' efforts
are most appropriately directed. Are efforts devoted to the development of reflection in individuals futile without also devoting a substantial effort to the educational insitutions in which the student teachers'
practice will hopefully be further developed? Are reflective teaching
programs more appropriately directed to groups of inservice teachers in
schools where sustained professional support is more feasible?

These are some of the many issues that require to be addressed in examining
the role and potential of reflective teaching; and which are examined to
varying degrees by the chapters of this book.

Organization of the Book

The contributions to this book arose from a conference on Conceptualizing
Reflection in Teacher Development, held at the University of Bath in 1991.

Each of the chapters is concerned with exploring the concept of reflection and considering its contribution to teacher education. The papers range across different stages of professional development, some focusing particularly on preservice education, others on inservice or professional development generally. Some of the chapters are concerned with particular strategies for promoting reflection and how they might operate in a teacher education context, others dwell more upon a theoretical appreciation of how reflection features in the processes of professional development, and how it relates to issues of quality in teacher education.

In Chapter 1, Linda Valli analyzes seven preservice education programs in the US that have been designed around the notion of the reflective teacher. This analysis provides a useful descriptive base, illustrating the wide range of conceptions of reflection that have developed in teacher education and how these have come to be used to inform program design. Valli, however, also uses her analysis to highlight teacher educators' predominant concern with the *processes* of reflection (in particular, how student teachers think about classroom practice), warning that the *content* of reflection (what student teachers reflect upon) deserves equal attention from teacher educators to avoid reflection becoming trivialized or narrowly focused on instructional strategies to the exclusion of wider issues concerning educational purposes, principles and ethics. Valli also raises the issue of conceptualizing quality in reflection, suggesting that preservice teacher education programs require teacher educators to make judgments about quality in student teachers' reflection. There may, for instance, be a developmental process of becoming reflective, a process through which students gradually improve in their reflectiveness. Judgments about such quality, however, probably demand more sophisticated concepts of reflection than are commonly used at present, and Valli draws particular attention to the attitudinal and emotional dimensions of reflection that have commonly been ignored in the teacher education context.

It is the development of a more sophisticated concept of reflection that is the focus of the paper by Vicki LaBoskey. Drawing upon a wide range of literature and her own empirical research, LaBoskey develops a framework for thinking about reflection in terms of a complex interplay of cognitive abilities, beliefs, values, attitudes and emotions which are employed within a problem-solving context. By mapping out the personal and contextual variables that influence reflection in teacher education, LaBoskey provides a means of thinking about how reflective practice might be encouraged in teacher education, and how the 'common-sense thinker' may be helped to develop their cognitive and affective capabilities to reflect.

Chapter 3 is also concerned with how greater levels of reflection can be achieved with student teachers. Donald McIntyre points out that while many approaches to encouraging reflection, and in particular action research, seem to have been effective at increasing student teachers' awareness of their own practice and raising questions about practice at a technical level, they have generally failed in their attempts to increase student teachers' awareness of the moral, ethical and political contexts of their practice. McIntyre argues that the development of such awareness and an ability to analyze educational practice in a wider context is dependent on a theoretical appreciation of education, and he points towards the important role of academic theory and empirical research as tools to facilitate and expand the student teacher's reflective capabilities. McIntyre suggests that at a time when teacher education is under some political pressure to become more 'practical', it is important to recognize the contribution that theoretical and research knowledge can make to the professional development of teachers.

Sarah Tann examines the contribution of reflective writing to the professional development of student teachers. She suggests that reflective writing is a means of making explicit one's own personal theories and thereby making them more accessible to analysis and evaluation. In a study of thirty-two student teachers' lesson evaluations, she identified a developmental trend in which students moved from partial descriptions and unsubstantiated judgments to a greater frankness, open-mindedness and ability to link personal theories to public theories and research evidence and a willingness to search for alternative explanations. Tann extracts from this a number of tutoring strategies that might help student teachers to develop a language for describing their practice and a conceptual framework for analyzing it.

Chapter 5 also focuses on the contribution of reflective writing to student teachers' professional development. Gary Knowles discusses the value of extended diaries or personal histories as a means of helping student teachers become aware of their own values and beliefs, their ways of thinking about teaching and learning and the impact of their own life histories in shaping their perspectives on teaching. Whilst, like Tann, Knowles argues that such techniques help student teachers to make their taken-for-granted beliefs explicit to provide a starting point for reflection, he also argues for the importance of dialogue journals in which tutors and teachers can respond to students' accounts, providing alternative interpretations and responses to students' writing that encourage them to question and analyze their perspectives.

Anne Proctor suggests that an important contribution to the promotion of reflection in teacher education is the work of the supervising tutor. Whilst several theoretical models for supervision have recently been prescribed for how tutors might constructively supervise their students, Proctor suggests that tutors have difficulty in adopting such models and that improvements to the quality of supervision practices need to build more upon an understanding of what supervisors actually do in their work. Proctor's own study of supervision practices indicates the areas of judgment that contribute to the assessments and feedback offered by tutors, but also points towards considerable idiosyncrasy in what tutors attend to. If tutors are to take a more active role in promoting reflection, Proctor suggests that they need themselves to become more reflective, to share their judgments about practice with others and to subject them to greater critical scrutiny.

One of the areas where one might expect teachers' thinking to develop is in the area of pupils' learning. One might reasonably expect the beliefs teachers hold about pupils as learners to influence the ways in which they plan lessons, how they structure and pace activities and how they interact with individual children. In a study of eleven different teacher education programs, covering preservice, induction, inservice and alternate programs in which teachers were required to reflect upon their own beliefs and question their assumptions about children's learning, Bill McDiarmid examined the changes that occurred in teachers' beliefs about such matters as innate mathematical and literary abilities and the source of pupil success and failure in school. McDiarmid found considerable diversity in teachers' views, and perhaps surprisingly, that these views seemed to change very little as a result of training.

Tom Russell poses some challenging questions about the role of reflection in learning to teach and questions the relationship that is frequently assumed to exist between reflection and the quality of teaching. Russell goes on to suggest that reflection is concerned with 'learning from experience' rather than 'learning from words', the latter being the form of learning with which students are often more familiar. Russell then goes on to suggest that we might learn most about reflection from helping those students who are slow to learn to teach and who experience difficulty, since these are the students who grapple with the task of reflection.

Finally, Anne Edwards and David Brunton consider the role of reflection in inservice education for teachers, focusing particularly on the contribution of action research to teachers' professional development. They argue that the rhetoric of action research frequently draws attention to the empowerment of teachers, the development of teachers' own pedagogic discourse and the taking of control over their own professional development. They suggest, however, that all too often action research studies are limiting because teachers fail to extend their own thinking or to interact with a public discourse. Edwards and Brunton draw upon Vygotskian theory to understand the processes of learning from action research and conclude that there is a crucial role for the external change agent or mentor. The role of the mentor may well alter at different stages of the action research cycle, but serves both to introduce teachers to the discourse of practice and to evaluate it critically, contributing to its further development.

Understanding the Role of Reflection in the Professional Education of Teachers

The papers highlight several issues that require much further exploration, but they also point towards some common themes. Several papers, for instance, begin to identify the distinctive and complex nature of the reflection involved in learning to teach. Reflection in teacher education, it is suggested, involves values, attitudes and beliefs as well as cognitive skills. The processes of learning to teach, focused as they are on the analysis and development of experience, may be in marked contrast to the academic learning to which student teachers may have been more accustomed.

A second common feature emerging from the papers is that there appears to be a developmental process in becoming reflective. In the early stages of preservice education, student teachers need to develop a vocabulary for talking, writing and thinking about practice and, at this stage, simply being able to describe practice may well be a significant achievement. Thereafter, reflection may develop into making explicit underlying beliefs and assumptions and also using other public knowledge such as research evidence and academic theories or teaching principles by which to appraise classroom practice and its context. Such processes appear to apply both to student teachers and also to more experienced teachers.

A third feature emphasized in several chapters is that we may frequently have overly high expectations for the achievements of student teachers. When teacher educators expect student teachers to conduct insightful and analytical evaluations of their lessons, for instance, this may well be a very high-level demand to which few students are able to respond. Changes in student teachers', and even experienced teachers', levels of reflection appear to occur only over fairly lengthy periods of time.

A danger raised by some of the papers is that of making reflection too process oriented. Reflection for its own sake may be unconstructive and even debilitating. The content and the context of reflection are also of importance, and these considerations ought to inform the design of the teacher education curriculum.

Finally, the studies reported in this book repeatedly emphasize the role of the mentor, teacher educator or change agent — the person who acts as facilitator in the development of reflection. What characterizes the facilitator is their mastery of a public language for describing practice and the learning of teachers, their ability to engage in constructive dialogue with teachers about their work, to help teachers take charge of their own learning and their willingness to withdraw their support at appropriate times so that teachers develop their own independence.

The papers in this book go some way towards illuminating popular debates about the contribution of reflection to teacher education. In doing so, inevitably they pose further questions and identify further areas for research and development. Collectively, however, they point towards a view of professional growth which recognizes teaching as a complex activity that is highly demanding both cognitively and affectively and is a process of continuous development in which teachers themselves have a high personal as well as professional investment, working as they do in a context of powerful ideological and physical constraints. It is through a greater understanding of this professional growth through reflection that many researchers, teacher educators and teachers are currently seeking to improve the quality of education in our schools.

References

CALDERHEAD, J. (1992) 'Dilemmas in Developing Reflective Teaching', *Teacher Education Quarterly.*

CALDERHEAD, J. and ROBSON, M. (1991) 'Images of Teaching: Student Teachers' Early Conceptions of Classroom Practice', *Teaching and Teacher Education*, 7, 1–8.

CARR, W. and KEMMIS, S. (1986) *Becoming Critical*, Lewes, Falmer Press.

DEWEY, J. (1933) *How We Think*, Boston: D.C. Heath and Co.

KOLB, D.A. (1984) *Experiential Learning: experience as the source of learning and development*, Englewood Cliffs, N.J.: Prentice Hall.

KORTHAGEN, F.A.J. (1988) 'The influence of learning orientations on the development of reflective teaching', in CALDERHEAD, J. (ed.) *Teachers Professional Learning*, Lewes: Falmer Press.

SCHÖN, D.A. (1983) *The Reflective Practitioner*, London: Temple Smith.

ZEICHNER, K.M. and LISTON, D.P. (1987) 'Teaching student teachers to reflect', *Harvard Educational Review*, 57, 23–48.

1   Reflective Teacher Education Programs: An Analysis of Case Studies

Linda R. Valli

In 1987 some teacher educators who were working on sponsored projects to improve teacher preparation met to plan a conference on reflection.[1] One of the things we discussed at that initial meeting was evidence of improved student reflectivity. When asked about the program at my own university I responded that while most student teachers focused their reflection on issues of classroom control and instructional delivery, some were beginning to explore broader issues such as gender equity.

The quizzical reaction of my colleagues made me realize that my construction of the issue was different from theirs. After more dialogue, I realized that my frame of reference was what I later called a sociological perspective, while theirs was a psychological perspective (Valli and Taylor, 1989). I, in other words, used the expanding scope or content of students' inquiry as evidence of improved reflection: What were students concerned about? What type of school or classroom problem mattered to them? My colleagues, on the other hand, had a more psychological perspective. They focused on the nature or quality of reflection: did we have evidence that inquiry-oriented teacher education programs improved student thinking? That programs increased the complexity and sophistication of their reflective processes?

In this chapter I explore the question of reflectivity by examining how seven teacher education programs in the United States deal with these content and quality issues.[2] I am not looking at what students learn from the programs, but, more simply, at what the programs themselves espouse as their goals and values.[3] My approach is deliberately reductionist. I am looking primarily for commonalities, characteristics which programs mutually share; other authors have closely examined program differences (see Valli, 1992).

The cases were chosen because they represent a range of institutions in the United States which have given serious attention to program development and about which written materials were available.[4] They represent public and private institutions, four- and five-year programs, undergraduate and graduate programs and alternative programs. Some programs are organized generically across grade and content areas; others maintain the traditional divisions between elementary and secondary preparation. Many have received state or federal grants and all represent attempts to incorporate reflection throughout professional preparation rather than in just a few courses or field experiences.

This programmatic level of intervention stands in marked contrast to attempts generally made to teach reflection. In a review of inquiry-oriented teacher education, Tom (1985) uses few examples which incorporate reflection throughout the various components of the professional education sequence. Instead, his examples come from particular strategies devised to promote reflection, from individual foundations or methods courses whose instructors choose to implement reflection, or from advocacy literature in which authors argue for some type of inquiry orientation in the preparation of teachers.

Zeichner (1987) similarly found that 'most inquiry-oriented teacher educators have sought to prepare more reflective teachers by altering specific courses or program components within an overall program context which remains unchanged' (p. 567). Yet this piecemeal approach generally fails to influence the perspectives of teacher candidates. For that type of impact, a more intense, coherent framework is necessary (Zeichner, 1987). As Barnes (1987) claims, 'learning to teach, like any other complicated activity, requires building schemata that are well-organized and capable of directing one's actions as a teacher' (p. 14). Such schemata building can only be accomplished over time in programs which reinforce and build upon prior learning in a coherent and systematic manner.

Before proceeding, one concept important to the content and quality of reflective teaching needs to be introduced, the concept of a *technical* orientation to teaching. As used in the reflection literature, the term technical has actually developed dual meanings which have not been explicitly identified or separated. The first construction of technical has implications for the content or scope of reflection, the second for the equality of reflection.

In the first construction, technical refers to the means of accomplishing a particular goal. It embodies an instrumentalist orientation to teaching wherein 'the primary concern is with fostering the development of skill in an actual performance of a predetermined task' (Zeichner, 1983, p. 4). In an instrumental orientation, reflective questions focus on making the teaching/learning process more effective and efficient (Van Manen, 1977). They address the means or procedures for delivering education while leaving important questions about the purposes, values and goals of schooling unexamined. In this sense of technical, the *scope of reflection* is restricted to the *means* of managing classrooms and delivering instruction. Technically reflective teachers would be concerned with such questions as: Was the class under control? Am I moving through the curriculum in a timely fashion? They would not question whether the curriculum was *worth* getting through or what harm certain behavioral techniques might cause.

Implied in this definition is a second meaning of technical: using knowledge in a straightforward way to direct practice. As Grimmett *et al.* (1990) describe it, in a technical approach to reflection 'propositional knowledge is reflected upon and then applied to practice in an instrumental manner' (p. 25). Teachers are urged to conform their practice to generalizations from empirical research (Grimmett, 1990; Tom and Valli, 1990). At times, as in state-mandated evaluation, this takes the form of reflecting on rules of practice. Since most of these rules or generalizations are derived from research on teaching, the focus of teachers' attention again would be on generic issues of teaching, learning and classroom management. Under this meaning of technical, *quality of reflection* would be simply determined by the ability to match teaching behavior to the established codes.

As we shall see, neither of these uses of technical has predominately guided the development of the teacher education programs described in this chapter.[5] Although there is considerable variation among the programs, technical approaches have been rejected as overly narrow in scope (unduly limiting the content of reflection) and as vesting too much authority and control in externally-derived research knowledge (adversely affecting the quality of reflection). Instead, the cases I analysed could be described as deliberative and dialectical modes of reflection (Grimmett *et al.*, 1990).[6]

In deliberative reflection, knowledge about teaching is relativistic, dependent on context, and is used to inform, not direct, practice. It is similar to what McCarthy *et al.* (1989) call strategic reflection, in which problems in teaching are examined from several practical and philosophic perspectives before a decision is reached on a particular course of action. In dialectical reflection, externally-derived knowledge about teaching is less important. Instead, reflection is more personally grounded and is used to apprehend and transform experience.

More will be said about these approaches to reflection in the next two sections. After examining the content and quality of reflection in the seven programs, I look at these two concepts in relation to one another and then explore what aspects of reflection are missing from the programs. The chapter ends with a cautionary note about instructional strategies.

The Question of Reflective Content

One way of analyzing the reflective content of teacher education programs is to use Tom's (1985) notion of arenas of the problematic. Tom specifies four arenas of the teaching situation, arranged by degrees of comprehensiveness, which can be subjected to doubt, inquiry and reflection. Moving from the small to the large, these arenas are the teaching-learning process, subject matter knowledge, political and ethical principles underlying teaching, and educational institutions within their broad social context.

Although none of the programs makes only the teaching/learning process problematic, most put primary emphasis on this smallest arena. The content they specify for reflection is instruction, instructional design, individual differences, group processes and dynamics, research on teaching, learning, motivation, effective teaching behaviors, discipline and classroom organization. The Masters Certification program at the University of Maryland, for example, has identified four arenas of inquiry as: research on teaching on effective psychology, models of teaching and research on effective schools (McCaleb, Borko, and Arends, 1992). The Reflective Inquiry Teacher Education (RITE) program at the University of Houston asks students to analyze different classroom management styles by having them record teacher time allocation, student time on task, and student-teacher interaction patterns (Clift, Houston, and McCarthy, 1992). There is discussion in other programs of the new paradigm on how students learn and the set of pedagogical principles which inform teachers' work. Given the difficulties beginning teachers have with discipline and classroom disorder (Veenman, 1984), this focus on the teaching-learning process is not surprising.

Secondary emphasis is placed on the broader arenas — ethical principles and social context — by including such topics as normative influences on schooling, cultural diversity and social forces which impinge on teacher decision-making. At Catholic University, faculty have developed a conceptual framework for the purpose of expanding the scope of students' reflection to these broader arenas (Ciriello, Valli, and Taylor, 1992). This framework consists of three dimensions: Schwab's (1973) curriculum commonplaces, van Manen's (1977) modes of reflection, and Berlak and Berlak's (1981) dilemmas of schooling. The Academically Talented Teacher Education Program (ATTEP) at Kent State University teaches students to use psychological, sociological and critical modes of inquiry to question teaching practice, make reasoned choices, and engage in complex problem-solving (Applegate and Shaklee, 1992). The three modes of inquiry guide the core seminars which ATTEP students take. Inquiry into Learning is guided by a psychological perspective, Research in Teaching by a sociological perspective, and Inquiry into Schooling by a critical perspective. A number of universities explicitly incorporate critical inquiry through which students must reflect on social and ethical aspects of schooling. At the University of Maryland, which has had a strong orientation toward research on teaching, a shift toward a more radical critique of schooling is underway.

Stating that programs have a primary and secondary emphasis, however, as though they deal with these issues as separate content areas, is misleading. If they did, in fact, put separate and primary emphasis on the teaching/learning arena, they should be described as having a technical orientation since they would be focusing on the means of delivering instruction. But the programs do not do this. They include the broader arenas by relating them to the teaching-learning process. They teach students that instructional decisions are context dependent and that educational practice must be related to normative questions about the purpose and goals of schooling. In the Multiple Perspectives program at Michigan State University, for example, students consider how the various functions of schooling (academic outcomes, personal responsibility, social responsibility and social justice) can cause conflict within a teacher's role and demand wise professional judgment. The program deliberately includes different levels of reflection (technical, clinical, personal and critical) to help prospective teachers relate these functions and develop their thinking (Putnam and Grant, 1992). Personal reflection, for instance, helps teacher candidates develop a professional sense of self and use that knowledge to create humane class-room environments.

So reflection on issues of teaching and learning does not occur in a vacuum but within broader questions of purposes, goals, values and constraints. In these programs, the teaching-learning process is best depicted not on one end of a continuum, but rather as a small circle within the larger circles of ethical principles and social institutions. This connection of the smaller arenas of the problematic to the larger supports Brennan and Noffke's (1988) finding from action research projects that concerns about management and discipline often embody 'the whole area of teacher-student relationships' and provide a way to help prospective teachers consider the interconnectedness and ethical base of classroom issues (p. 6). This connection removes these programs from a strictly technical orientation to teacher preparation since reflection focuses on more than just the instrumental means of instructional delivery. As one set of authors put it; 'Our vision of teacher as decision-maker challenges the orthodoxy of a single knowledge base where ends are undisputed and means are empirically revealed' (Oja, *et al.*, 1992).

One minor theme which does not fall explicitly into any of the four arenas was also evident in three programs, the theme of self as teacher which includes personal teaching styles, themes, or theories; professional growth; or, as one program calls it: 'an effective teaching personality' (Clift, Houston, and McCarthy, 1992). The focus here is on reflection for self-enlightenment: confronting the self to examine feelings and emotions about teaching, students and the school setting (McCarthy, *et al.*, 1989). The term 'co-explorers' is used in the University of New Hampshire program to highlight the importance of making a methodological commitment to listen to the experience of others, to try to understand others in their own terms, and to expect to have the same effort made on their own behalf (Oja, *et al.*, 1992). This theme suggests a strong developmental perspective: the personal construction of meaning in becoming a teacher. It is an example of the dialectical mode of reflection mentioned earlier. In this mode of reflection, official research knowledge as a guide to action is de-emphasized. Rather, students are urged to draw upon personal knowledge to transform or recon-struct their experience.

Linda Valli

The Question of Reflective Quality

A different way of looking at issues of reflection embedded in teacher education programs is to examine what is regarded as reflective quality. This psychological orientation to reflection is rooted in the conceptual development work of Perry (1968), Kitchener and King (1981), and others which indicates that considerable growth in thinking occurs during the college years.

Although much research has been done in this area, none of these seven teacher education programs assumes the formidable task of improving conceptual level as an indicator of students' reflective qualities. They do not explicitly try to move students from dualistic (right or wrong) to relativistic levels of thinking. Rather, they use more modest indicators directly related to program goals and strategies such as avoiding unthinking conformity, analyzing a problem from multiple perspectives, and using new evidence to reassess professional judgments.

Like content for reflection, where the teaching-learning process was the main emphasis, one predominent theme emerged from analyzing what program developers consider to be quality of reflection. While programs variously address the need for 'scholarly' reflection, different modes of inquiry, consideration of alternative explanations, and so forth, these indicators of reflective quality all point to the theory/practice relationship. They are all ways of problematizing this relation. What counts as quality of reflection is the ability to make the relationship between theory and practice problematic.

As mentioned earlier, using research knowledge to guide practice in a straightforward way is not valued by these programs. The programs present a more complex view of the knowledge-practice relation. With Schön (1983), they reject the concept of technical rationality, or 'instrumental problem-solving made rigorous by the application of scientific theory and technique' (p. 21). Students are encouraged to explore the tentativeness and tenuousness of the theory/practice relation. They are taught that decision-making is dependent upon interrelationships among principles from various disciplines and that teacher decisions must balance competing demands and expectations placed on the school: demands, for example, that simultaneously promote academic learning, personal and social responsibility, and appreciation for diverse learners. In a program which emphasizes research and developing scholar teachers, students are taught the need for dialogue between theory and practice and the importance of not blindly translating research into a set of recipes and formulas (McCaleb, Borko, and Arends, 1992). They are encouraged to avoid unthinking conformity and the unexamined adoption of research findings. Distinction is made between research findings (the way things work in general) and practice (the uniqueness of each classroom setting and event).

A number of universities explicitly frame their programs within contextual questions of the goals of schooling. Catholic University uses Berlak and Berlak's (1981) concept of dilemmas of teaching to relate research findings to value orientations and judgments made about particular students in particular situations. The Professional Teacher Program (PROTEACH) at the University of Florida uses a research course and seminar not merely to expose students to process/product research, but to introduce them to the historical context of education research and conflicting research traditions. Students have to formulate for themselves an answer to the question: 'What is the role of research in teaching practice?' (Ross, Johnson, and Smith, 1992). By definition, such framing problematizes the theory/practice relation.

In other programs students are encouraged to develop an 'intuitive feel for what is right and wrong' rather than follow a prescriptive orientation and are initiated into what has been traditionally called 'the art and craft of teaching.' The emphasis on art and craft at Kent State University is striking since ATTEP was designed as an alternative with a research focus for exceptionally strong undergraduate students. And as a final example, the University of New Hampshire program encourages cooperating teachers to study and use alternative models of supervision based on adult development theory. The clear implication in this program model is that supervisors do not guide practice by using a knowledge base checklist, but rather by assessing a teacher's developmental characteristics and needs.

The theory/practice relation in each of these examples is thus problematized. The reflective question is not primarily: 'Did I employ such and such aspect of research?' but 'Is that theory or finding relevant to this situation and do I accept the value assumptions implicit in that strand of research?' In fact, when programs found that certain strategies or instruments inadvertently promoted technical thinking, they discontinued their use.

So instead of being technical, the relation between theory and practice embedded in these cases is what Grimmett *et al.* (1990) refer to as deliberative and dialectical modes of reflective knowing. Contrasted with a technical mode of knowing which directs action through reflection on research-based knowledge, the deliberative and dialectical modes view the purpose of reflection in a more complex light: as *informing* action by deliberation on competing views or as *transforming* action by reconstructing personal experience.

This does not mean, however, that research-based knowledge is discounted and only common sense and personal experience is used as a source for reflective practice. On the contrary, the programs described here place considerable, albeit different, degrees of emphasis on the knowledge base(s) for teaching. In one program, research is one of three interrelated themes. In others, it is specified as the content for reflection. Thus we have what Tom (1985) would call a disciplined, as opposed to a merely common-sense, approach to inquiry, an approach which entails 'the application of concepts, theories and research strategies drawn from the humanities and the social sciences' (p. 39). Teacher educators in these programs seem to be wrestling with the dilemma of how to balance or relate research knowledge with personal knowledge.

Discussion

Because of the conversation I mentioned at the beginning of this paper about reflective evidence, I began this analysis expecting to find some programs which valued or primarily attended to either the content of student reflection or the quality of their reflection. I was pleasantly surprised to discover that this is not the case. Each program attends to both aspects of reflection and, from the materials I had, it was hard to determine if one is more highly valued than the other. This might be because, as I came to discover, the distinction between quality and content of reflection is not as absolute as I originally thought.

The reason I draw this conclusion is that while the theory/practice relation is used as a way of improving reflective quality, the relation can also be regarded as the central problem, the central content of these programs. Tom's four arenas of the problematic are not the only possibilities. As mentioned earlier, the self as developing professional is an additional arena. But the theory/practice relation functions as an overarching category encompassing all others. When students use deliberative or dialectical rather than technical modes of reflection to interrogate issues within the various arenas, they are examining not just the arenas but the relation between theory and practice as well.

To summarize thus far, the concepts of content and quality of reflection were helpful in identifying the two dominant themes of these programs: 1) viewing technical issues in relation to larger ones and 2) problematizing the theory/practice relation. The minor theme of self as developing professional also emerged from the analysis. The major themes represent a deliberative mode of reflection; the minor theme represents a dialectical mode.[7]

But in addition to these 'present' themes, the concepts of content and quality also permitted 'absent' themes to be identified. Under content of reflection the one arena of the problematic which received little attention is subject matter knowledge. One program does use the image of 'scholar teacher' and another does relate academic learning to other goals of schooling. But in none of the programs were students strongly encouraged to reject a taken-for-granted view of subject matter and engage 'in a long-term study of the subtleties of fundamental bodies of knowledge' (Tom, 1985, p. 38). The programs did not problematize subject matter knowledge in this way.

Two absences were identified under the quality of reflection: reflective attitudes, and intuition or emotions. Although programs might consider reflective attitudes to be tacit goals of their programs, only two explicitly articulate their significance. One program discusses the importance of instilling in students the attitude that learning to teach is a life-long process;

another emphasizes the importance of fostering the desire for continuous professional growth. Given the long-standing literature on reflection being more than a set of skills, it is surprising that this is not a more dominant theme. Perhaps the amorphous nature of attitudes and the difficulty of developing or changing attitudes accounts for the relatively slight attention given this area.

Emphasizing the role of emotions and intuition in reflectivity is another missing area. Although one program mentions the art of teaching, only one uses the term intuition and encourages students to use both intellectual and emotional resources in reflecting on the meaning and effect of their teaching. Other programs seem to value strict rationality, omitting intuition and emotions entirely (see Ross, Johnson, and Smith, 1992). As Houston and Clift (1990) hypothesize: 'current definitions of reflection are strongly influenced by the Western cultural heritage, which emphasizes analysis and problem-solving as opposed to negotiation, contemplation or enlightenment. . . . [They are influenced by] the importance of an analytical method that stresses objectivity and emotional detachment' (p. 211).

Conclusion

Before concluding, one other dimension, the *process* of reflection, bears mentioning as a major, valued focus. Written descriptions of the programs have considerable detail on the strategies used to foster reflection. The three primary strategies used across the programs are journal-keeping, seminar dialogues, and action research projects. While specifying the strategies used to develop reflective orientations is essential if program goals are to be realized, a potential danger resides in valuing, or over-valuing, process.

A process focus could detract from more central questions of the purpose, content and quality of reflection. How to get students to reflect can take on a life of its own, can become *the* programmatic goal. What students reflect on can become immaterial. Racial tension as a school issue, for instance, could become no more or less worthy of reflection than field trips or homework assignments. Quality of reflection could also be neglected if instructional strategies are not explicitly derived from program goals. Should process become the dominant concern, programs would become technical, in the most limited sense of that orientation, since they would focus more on the instrumental means than on the normative ends of teacher preparation.

Furthermore, many of these strategies are now so common that they could easily be used non-reflectively, apart from any unified image of a reflective teacher, theoretical position, or conceptual framework. So while the programs discussed in this chapter have clear teacher images, specified knowledge bases, and detailed expectations for reflective quality, instructional strategies could inadvertently become the guiding force of programs, ultimately undermining their coherence, unless they are carefully linked to these more central aspects of reflection.

Notes

1 This working conference on Reflection in Teaching and Teacher Education was sponsored by the University of Houston and the United States Department of Education, Office of Educational Research and Improvement (OERI) and was held in Houston in October 1987. One outcome of the conference was the publication of Renee Clift, W. Robert Houston, Marleen Pugach (eds), *Encouraging Reflective Practice in Education*, New York: Teachers College Press, 1990.

2 The seven programs analyzed in this paper are the Multiple Perspectives program at Michigan State University, the PROTEACH program at the University of Florida, the RITE program at the University of Houston, ATTEP at Kent State University, the Masters Certification program at the University of Maryland, the five-year program at the University of New Hampshire, and the elementary teacher education program at the Catholic University of America. For full case description as well as six critique chapters see L. Valli (1992).

3 Calderhead (1992) raises the important question about what and how much prospective teachers can learn about being reflective during their preservice years. While these seven programs have all made initial attempts to answer these questions, much is still uncertain. We know more about how students function in their preparation years than in their beginning years of teaching.

4 Although written descriptions of programs are insufficient, and often inaccurate, portrayals of the enacted curriculum, they are excellent indicators of what faculty perceive to be important — of what aspects of curriculum they value.

5 Berliner (1988), however, offers a strong argument for the technical preparation of prospective teachers. He advocates a focus on following scripted lessons and practising classroom routines during the preservice years, leaving the development of more complex skills such as decision-making and priority-setting to somewhere around the third year of teaching.

6 In a critique of these programs, Sparks-Langer (1992) similarly determined that most were framed within, what she calls, cognitive and critical approaches. Using the concept of traditions of reflective teaching practice to critique the chapters, Zeichner (1992) came to a somewhat different conclusion. He argues that although some programs incorporate an emphasis on the social context of schooling, a social efficiency orientation is dominant. I believe that the differences in these two analyses result from several factors: a) giving more or less weight to the various pieces of evidence, b) using different analytic categories or lenses, and c) defining categories differently (e.g. more broadly or narrowly). For instance, Zeichner (1992) includes deliberative approaches within his social efficiency tradition while Grimmett *et al.* (1990) place developmental and social re-constructionist approaches in a dialectical category. Of related interest is that, in a separate analysis, Feiman-Nemser (1990) uses one of the seven programs (PROTEACH) as an example of a technological orientation. Sparks-Langer sees it as critical, and Zeichner calls it mostly developmentalist. In actual practice, PROTEACH probably has strong strands of each of these orientations. Since programs have histories and are constantly changing, no one claims that they are pure types. These analytic differences, then, are not totally surprising.

7 On an interesting side note, faculty in some programs view different conceptualizations of reflection as a problem to be overcome while others deliberately structure different conceptualizations into their programs. The RITE and

Multiple Perspectives programs provide a vivid contrast on this issue. In a recent review of Liston and Zeichner's *Teacher Education and the Social Conditions of Schooling*, Tom (1991) raises the same issue. While Liston and Zeichner argue that one particular reform tradition should influence the direction of change in teacher education, Tom argues that a synthesis of reform traditions would be better.

References

APPLEGATE, J. and SHAKLEE, B. (1992) 'Stimulating reflection while learning to teach', in VALLI, L. (ed.) *Reflective teacher education: Cases and critiques*, New York: SUNY.

BARNES, H. (1987) 'The conceptual basis for thematic teacher education programs', *Journal of Teacher Education*, **38**(4), pp. 13–18.

BERLAK, A. and BERLAK, H. (1981) *Dilemmas of schooling*, London: Methuen.

BERLINER, D. (1988) *The development of expertise in pedagogy*, Washington DC: AACTE Publications.

BRENNAN, M. and NOFFKE, S. (1988) 'Reflection in student teaching: The place of data in action research'. A paper prepared for presentation at the annual meeting of the American Educational Research Association, New Orleans.

CALDERHEAD, J. (1992) 'The role of reflection in learning to teach', in VALLI, L. (ed.) *Reflective teacher education: Cases and critiques*, New York: SUNY.

CIRIELLO, M., VALLI, L. and TAYLOR, N. (1992) 'Problem solving is not enough', in VALLI, L. (ed.) *Reflective teacher education: Cases and critiques*, New York: SUNY.

CLIFT, R., HOUSTON, W.R. and McCARTHY, J. (1992) 'Getting it RITE: A case of negotiated curriculum in teacher preparation', in VALLI, L. (ed.) *Reflective teacher education: Cases and critiques*, New York: SUNY.

FEIMEN-NEMSER, S. (1990) 'Teacher preparation: Structural and conceptual alternatives', in HOUSTON, W.R. (ed.) *Handbook of research on teacher education*, New York: MacMillan, pp. 212–33.

GRIMMETT, P., MACKINNON, A., ERICKSON, G. and RIECKEN, T. (1990) 'Reflective practice in teacher education', in CLIFT, R.T., HOUSTON, W.R. and PUGACH, M. (eds) *Encouraging reflective practice: An analysis of issues and programs*, New York: Teachers College Press, pp. 20–38.

HOUSTON, W.R. and CLIFT, R. (1990) 'The potential for research contributions to reflective practice', in CLIFT, R.T., HOUSTON, W.R. and PUGACH, M. (eds) *Encouraging reflective practice: An analysis of issues and programs*, New York: Teachers College Press, pp. 208–22.

KITCHENER, K. and KING, P. (1981) 'Reflective judgment concepts of justification and their relationship to age and education', *Journal of Applied Developmental Psychology*, **2**, pp. 89–116.

McCALEB, J., BORKO, H. and ARENDS, R. (1992) 'Reflections, research, and repertoire in the Masters certification program', in VALLI, L. (ed.) *Reflective teacher education: Cases and critiques*, New York: SUNY.

McCARTHY, J., CLIFT, R., BAPTISTE, H.P. and BAIN, L. (1989) 'Reflective inquiry teacher education faculty perceptions of change'. Paper presented at the annual meeting of the American Educational Research Association.

OJA, S., DILLER, A., CORCORAN, E. and ANDREW, M. (1992) 'Communities of inquiry, communities of support', in VALLI, L. (ed.) *Reflective teacher education: Cases and critiques*, New York: SUNY Press.

PERRY, W.G. (1970) *Forms of intellectual and ethical development in the college years: A scheme*, New York: Holt, Rinehart and Winston.

PUTNAM, J. and GRANT, S.G. (1992) 'Reflective practice in the Multiple Perspectives program', in VALLI, L. (ed.) *Reflective teacher education: Cases and critiques*, New York: SUNY Press.

ROSS, D., JOHNSON, M. and SMITH, W. (1992) 'Developing a PROfessional TEACHer', in VALLI, L. (ed.) *Reflective teacher education: Cases and critiques*, New York: SUNY Press.

SCHÖN, D. (1983) *The reflective practitioner*, New York: Basic Books.

SCHWAB, J. (1977) The practical 3: Translation into curriculum, *School Review*, **81**, pp. 501–22.

SPARKS-LANGER, G. (1992) 'In the eye of the beholder: Cognitive, critical and narrative approaches to teacher reflection', in VALLI, L. (ed.) *Reflective teacher education: Cases and critiques*, New York: SUNY Press.

TOM, A. (1985) 'Inquiring into inquiry-oriented teacher education', *Journal of Teacher Education*, **36**(5), pp. 35–44.

— (1991) 'Whither the professional curriculum for teachers', *The Review of Education*, **14**, pp. 21–30.

TOM, A.R. and VALLI, L. (1990) 'Professional knowledge for teachers, in HOUSTON, W.R. (ed.) *Handbook of research on teacher education*, New York: MacMillan, pp. 373–92.

VALLI, L. (ed.) (1992) *Reflective teacher education: Cases and critiques*, New York: SUNY Press.

VALLI, L. and TAYLOR, N.E. (1989) 'Evaluating a reflective teacher education model'. Paper presented at the Annual Meeting of the American Educational Research Association, San Francisco.

VAN MANEN, M. (1977) 'Linking ways of knowing with ways of being practical', *Curriculum Inquiry*, **6**(3), pp. 205–28.

VEENMAN, S. (1984) 'Perceived problems of beginning teachers', *Review of Educational Research*, **54**(2), pp. 143–78.

ZEICHNER, K. (1983) 'Alternative paradigms of teacher education', *Journal of Teacher Education*, **34**(3), pp. 3–9.

— (1987) 'Preparing reflective teachers: An overview of instructional strategies which have been employed in preservice teacher education', *International Journal of Educational Research*, **11**(5), pp. 565–75.

— (1992) 'Conceptions of reflective teaching in contemporary US teacher education program reforms', in VALLI, L. (ed.) *Reflective teacher education: Cases and critiques*, New York: SUNY Press.

2   A Conceptual Framework for Reflection in Preservice Teacher Education

Vicki Kubler LaBoskey

In 1986 I embarked upon an extensive review of the literature on reflection and teacher education. As the Assistant Director of the Stanford Teacher Education Program my incentives were both practical and theoretical. I wanted to support the design and implementation of a reflective teacher education program and to evaluate and interpret the results of those efforts. The three bodies of literature that seemed most relevant to my concerns were: 1) discussions of the definition of reflection, particularly as it relates to teaching; 2) research on the structure and outcome of reflective teacher education programs; and 3) research and theory about learners and the learning process for groups and individuals (see LaBoskey, 1989).

What I discovered was that the meaning of reflection was not consistent among the theoreticians, researchers, or teacher educators who employed the term. As Calderhead (1989) observed in his review of the origins of the concept of 'reflective teaching', expressions used to refer to reflective processes in professional development 'disguise[d] a vast number of conceptual variations' (p. 2). I also found no single definition which seemed comprehensive enough to embrace all features potentially relevant to reflective teacher education. Thus, before I began systematically to investigate particular program structures and their outcomes, I needed to formulate my own conceptual framework. In this chapter I will describe first the definition which guided my initial studies. Then I will explicate a 'new' conceptual framework that evolved from further exploration of the literature and the results of my subsequent research. This conceptualization provides one comprehensive definition of reflection in preservice teacher education that can serve as guide for both practice and research.

The Initial Conceptual Framework

The initial conceptual framework can be seen in Figure 2.1. The review suggested, first, that novices do not enter teacher education programs as

Figure 2.1: *Reflection in preservice teacher education*

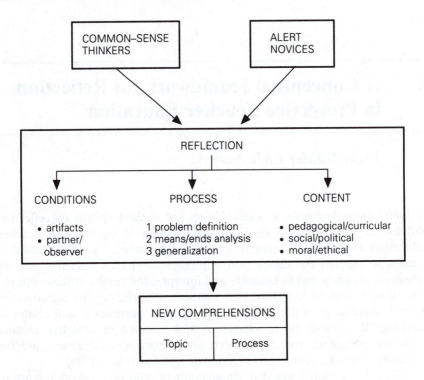

blank slates. After many years in classrooms, they have ideas about what teachers do. But these ideas were derived from a student perspective, not a teacher perspective, and thus are very likely to be inaccurate, inappropriate, or incomplete. Such misconceptions may distort or block any new information presented in the teacher education program. Consequently, teacher educators need to consider the potential influence of student preconceptions on the reflective activities and programs they design and implement.

Second, the review indicated that not all prospective teachers enter teacher education programs with the same views. Students vary in their pre-intervention beliefs, particularly in the degree of orientation toward growth and inquiry. That is, incoming students seem to differ in their location along a continuum of common-sense/pedagogical thinking (see Figure 2.2). Perhaps only those who begin closer to the pedagogical end of the continuum can benefit from a reflective education program. I defined the category of 'Alert Novice' to denote such students. They may not have the clear vision of what teaching is all about that the experienced Pedagogical Thinker does, but they seem to be headed in the right direction.

On the other hand, it may be that though the common-sense thinking of many preservice teachers is difficult to change, it is not impossible.

Figure 2.2:   Continuum for the reflective thinking of teachers

Common-sense Thinker	Alert Novice	Pedagogical
Self-orientation (Shift of attention from self or subject matter alone to what needs explaining to children) Short-term view Reliance on personal experience in learning to teach (learn by doing; trial and error) Metaphor of teacher as transmitter Unaware of need to learn; feeling of already knowing much from having been in classrooms as a student		Student-orientation Long-term view Differentiates teacher/learner roles Metaphor of teacher as facilitator Open to learning; growth-oriented Acknowledgement of need for conclusions to be tentative; need feedback and triangulation Means/ends thinking; awareness of teaching as a moral activity Strategic Imaginative Grounded in knowledge of self, children, and subject matter

'Common-sense Thinkers', when provided with very powerful reflective experiences that directly challenge misconceptions, may develop the capacity for pedagogical thinking. Though their initial thought processes may differ from Alert Novices or Pedagogical Thinkers, Common-sense Thinkers can become more like the others over time. Attention is turned, then, to the creation of programs and experiences capable of developing and encouraging reflection in student teachers with varying original preconceptions and modes of thinking.

Third, the review of the literature also suggested what some of the critical features of such programs and experiences may be. According to Dewey (1910), individuals must proceed through three steps of reflection: 1) problem definition; 2) means/ends analysis; and 3) generalization. He proposes that the process is initiated by a 'felt difficulty' which often requires a preliminary exploration of the problem. The individual must suspend judgment in this effort to diagnose accurately the situation. Once the problem has been defined, the person entertains a variety of suggestions as to how the problem might be solved. The implications of each proposal are explored through a reasoning process that selects relevant facts as evidence and applies appropriate principles to the interpretation of that data. When the results of the analysis show that one idea seems to account for the presenting conditions whereas the others do not, a tempered judgment can be made, terminating that particular act of reflection.

One problem with this model is that it tends to over-emphasize the procedures of logical thinking. I suggest that Dewey's attitudes of open-mindedness, responsibility and wholeheartedness are more critical to the reflective process than the specific steps. Though the stages do help to focus attention on potential aspects of the general process, they are not all necessary to each act of reflection. Any of the stages may be carried out reflectively or unreflectively. At any rate, teacher education programs may do well to provide novices with instruction and practice in the procedures and attitudes of reflective thinking.

When novices engage in this reflective process, they must reflect about something; there is a content to their reflection. Van Manen (1977) has defined three levels of reflectivity each of which implies a certain focus: 1) practical/technical; 2) social/political; and 3) moral/ethical. One problem with this conceptualization is that it implies a hierarchy that devalues the practical. Furthermore, this model overlooks many of teaching's more complex and comprehensive concerns in relation to instruction and curriculum. I suggest, therefore, that 'practical/technical' be changed to 'pedagogical/curricular', and that the categories be referred to as potential foci or content of reflection rather than levels. For any instance of reflection, each category is as important as the other. Because each is consequential, however, none should be entirely overlooked by the novice. They may reflect about one issue or more than one issue at a time and these issues can be from the same or different categories. The reflection may also include a consideration of the relationship between issues within or across categories. The implication is that teacher education programs should give attention to the nature and breadth of the topics requested and encouraged by their reflective assignments.

In addition, the review of the literature indicated that the content of reflection is influenced by the conditions of reflection. One suggestion is that preservice teachers need to interact with written records of their teaching and/or with partners who have observed their teaching. Second, a variety of artifactual and interactive components should be included in order to broaden the scope of the novices' reflective content. For any technique, the details, as they appear in particular situations, need attention and monitoring.

Finally, there were suggestions as to the outcomes of reflection in teacher education. The results of the acts of reflection engaged in by student teachers may be new comprehensions about a certain educational topic and/or about the process of reflection itself. If one aim of reflective teacher education programs is to help preservice teachers become reflective teachers, then one objective of the activities should be to teach the novices what it means to be reflective and how one goes about reflecting. Students can, therefore, gain new understandings about the skills and attitudes necessary for engaging in the reflective process. As they carry out these assignments, they will be reflecting upon some educational issue, idea or dilemma about which they may gain new insight. Thus, novices stand to acquire from their acts of reflection new comprehensions about an educational *topic* and about the *process* of reflection itself.

In summary, this conceptual framework conceives of reflection in preservice teacher education as an effort to transform any naive or problematic conceptions about teaching and learning held by entering students into those more conducive to pedagogical thinking. In the design and implementation of reflective teacher education programs, the process, content and conditions of reflective activity deserve consideration. But the preconceptions of student teachers differ and one way in which they may differ is in their degree of inquiry orientation. Those who enter with a fairly strong inquiry orientation I have called Alert Novices and those without Common-sense Thinkers. The same reflective activities are likely to be engaged in differently by these two groups, affecting the nature and content of any new comprehensions about topic and process that result from the enterprise.

The studies I have undertaken have been designed to test and refine various aspects of this definition. In particular I have tried to shed some light on the controversy about what reflection is and whether or not it can be taught by comparing the reflective processes and attitudes of prospective teachers with more and less initial reflective orientations. In the course of analyzing the results and returning to the literature for reconsideration, the framework has undergone several iterations, each incorporating more subtle distinctions and specific descriptors. Calderhead (1989) proposes that such a process may be a promising means for accomplishing the task:

> It is suggested that through an understanding of how student teachers do think about practice, why they think as they do, the substance of their thinking, how their thinking is affected by alternative course designs and how attempts to change their ways of thinking have been influential, we may develop an improved understanding of the nature and potential of reflection. (p. 9)

The definition incorporated into the 'new' conceptual framework is, in part, a result of an effort like that recommended by Calderhead. As I developed, through data analysis, an understanding of the thought processes of the student teacher participants, I was able to refine my definition of reflection. This had particular impact upon my depiction of preliminary student orientations (the conceptualizations of Common-sense Thinkers and Alert Novices) and of the potential outcomes of reflection.

The emerging patterns also revealed a need to incorporate more of the specifics already present in the literature. Therefore, changes were made to include direct treatment of each of four particular dimensions: purpose, context, procedure and content. In addition, the work in related disciplines

Figure 2.3: *'New' conceptual framework for reflection in preservice teacher education*

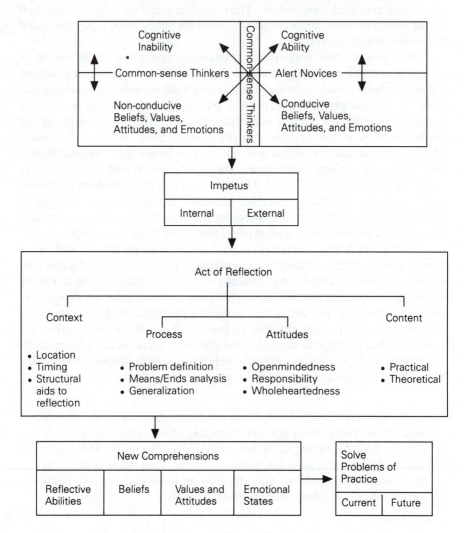

on emotions and moral values seemed to demand more explicit attention. Thus, these features were also built into the 'new' conceptual framework presented in Figure 2.3. As can be seen by comparing this with the original framework in Figure 1.1, the basic features and their relationships are still present; the fundamental components and guiding principles remain the same. In the next section I will explicate the 'new' conceptual framework and delineate how and why particular modifications were made.

The 'New' Conceptual Framework

The basic structure of the studies I have undertaken is as follows: a questionnaire is administered to all students entering a teacher education program in a given year. The responses are scored to obtain a measure of what I call, 'spontaneous reflectivity'. This term refers to situations where an inividual displays reflective thinking, or not, in response to an indirect question or circumstance. This is in contrast to situations where reflectivity is more explicitly structured into the requirements of the task, such as journal writing or action research. Individuals obtaining the lowest scores, the Common-sense Thinkers, and those with the highest scores, the Alert Novices, are then selected to be the subjects. Over the course of the preservice year a variety of data is gathered, such as pre- and post-questionnaires, audiotaped and transcribed interviews of student teachers and their supervisors, freewrite reactions to various educational experiences, professional journals, and course papers and projects. An example of the latter is an assignment I have called a case investigation. A case investigation is less rigorous and less extensive than a case study, but follows the same basic pattern. Thus, a case investigator is required to set a problem, gather data, analyze the data, and interpret the data for the purposes of reaching some conclusions about the problem set. All stages are then reported in a written document. I have used case investigations frequently in my work because they map well onto my notion of reflectivity and thus hold promise for both the promotion of reflective thinking and the documentation of those efforts. The data from all these sources are then analyzed through case studies to discover patterns of reflective processes and attitudes for the comparison groups and the individuals within those groups.

In one major study I conducted in 1989 the main source of data was a series of three different case investigations students produced during the first three-quarters of their preservice year. The case investigations were rated as Reflective, Unreflective, or Indeterminate using detailed sets of scoring criteria. Each case was also broken down into episodes associated with an aspect of reflective thinking — problem-setting, means/ends analysis, or generalization; each episode was also scored.

The results of this study were fourfold. First, the case investigation scores tended to support the position that initial reflectivity is resistant to change; 78 per cent of the cases written by Alert Novices were rated as Reflective in contrast to 22 per cent of the Common-sense Thinker cases. Second, within case scores were explored. Although certain features of case assignments seemed to be generally beneficial, the case structure alone was not as important as the interaction between the case and the person. Third, the case studies of each participant revealed differences in the thinking of individuals within and across groups. The Alert Novices were more likely than the Common-sense Thinkers to be guided by a strong belief, e.g. the need for active learning and personal interpretation on the part of students, which often served as a powerful impetus for reflection. This 'passionate creed', as I have called it, seemed to have some association with the novice's subject matter background. The two groups could also be differentiated by the nature of the questions they asked: Alert Novices tended to ask 'why' questions — 'Why am I doing what I am doing?' whereas the Common-sense Thinkers tended to ask 'how to' or 'what works' questions. In addition, results seemed to indicate that half of the Common-sense Thinkers were unreflective because of a cognitive inability and the other half because of an emotional interference. Thus, both ability and attitude appear to be necessary for reflective thinking. Fourth, as a result of a recursive process of data analysis and literature review, a 'new' conceptual framework for a comprehensive definition of reflection in preservice teacher education was proposed. It is this conceptualization that I will now describe by poinitng out the changes between it and the original conceptual framework.

The first distinctive feature of the 'new' conceptual framework is a more specific portrayal of the terms 'Common-sense Thinker' and 'Alert Novice'. The Common-sense Thinkers in my studies seemed to be categorized as such for two different reasons. Some appeared to be unable to engage in the cognitive process of reflective thinking. Others had the necessary cognitive abilities, but seemed to have beliefs, values, attitudes or emotions that prevented or distorted the reflective process in most situations. Thus, it appears that Alert Novices need to have both cognitive ability and conducive beliefs, values, attitudes and emotions. That is, those incoming preservice teachers who tend to engage in reflection with regularity in both 'spontaneous' and 'structured' situations may need to have both the ability and the propensity for doing so.

The cognitive abilities to which I am referring are those involved in the various stages of reflective thinking described by Dewey; those which might be categorized in the higher levels of Bloom's taxonomy: analysis, synthesis and evaluation. The reflective teacher must be able to describe and analyze the structural features of an educational situation, issue, or problem — problem definition; to gather and evaluate information as to the possible sources of the dilemma under consideration and to generate multiple alternative solutions and their potential implications — means/ends analysis; and to integrate all of the information into a tempered conclusion about or solution for the problem identified — generalization. The specific nature of these cognitive capacities is a topic for future research.

The results of this study further suggest that reflectivity does not only entail an 'intelligent' processing ability; it also includes a propensity for engaging in these reasoning activities. The evidence tends to support Dewey's proposal (1910) that the attitudes of openmindedness, responsibility and wholeheartedness are integral to reflective action. The individual needs to be willing and able to suspend judgment while actively searching for supporting and conflicting evidence and, when reaching a conclusion, to do so with temperance and a consideration of the potential short- and long-term consequences. The Alert Novices seem to be driven by a 'will to know', they are always on the lookout for something 'better'. In the words of one student teacher in this category, 'If I ever think that I know what I'm doing is right, I really want to step back and check my premise'. Alert Novices appear to value open exploration and continual growth. Their 'passionate creeds' and 'why' questions may be a part of these conducive beliefs, values, attitudes and emotions.

The non-conducive beliefs, values, attitudes and emotions of the Common-sense Thinkers may be due to an absence of 'passionate creeds' or to the asking of 'what works' rather than 'why' questions. Other evidence seems to indicate that interfering attitudes and emotions may also be operating. One Common-sense Thinker, for instance, seemed to feel that he was already a good teacher and did not need to reflect. Another may have been overwhelmed and distracted by the multiple requirements of her life, while a third's reflectivity about her teaching appeared to be confined to her lack of self-confidence. The work in emotions theory is supportive of these possibilities (Fridja, 1987; Izard, 1977; Leventhal and Scherer, 1987; Oatley and Johnson-Laird, 1987); this literature may prove useful in both understanding how the process functions and in developing means for resolving relevant problems.

Beliefs about teaching and the learning process also seem to be important. According to Kitchener's (1983; 1986) model, what one believes about knowledge and the knowing process influences the propensity for and means of engagement in reflection. Richert's (1987) research supports this notion: 'Preconceptions about reflection — what it is, how it might be useful, its relation to learning — all influence how teachers think about their work' (p. 176). There may also be a content aspect to this feature; for instance, the prospective teachers' beliefs about the structure of their discipline and their emotional attachment to it may have an impact on their thinking about the teaching of this area. The 'propositional knowledge' described by Shulman (1986) may be included here, or at least a tendency toward or openness to 'the norms, values, ideological or philosophical commitments of justice, fairness, equity and the like, that we wish teachers and those learning to teach to incorporate and employ' (p. 11).

This study tends to support the position of Boud, Keogh and Walker (1985) that the 'reflective process is a complex one in which both feelings and cognition are closely interrelated and interactive' (p. 11). If so, reflective teacher education programs cannot afford to overlook the association. Because these initial abilities and orientations seem to have a significant impact on how preservice teachers participate in the program's reflective structures and what they take away from them, the construction of a more complete picture of how these features look and function is an important topic for future research.

If a person is to engage in a particular act of reflection, there must be a reason or impetus for doing so; there must be a purpose to the endeavour.

According to Dewey, reflection begins with a 'felt difficulty' which can range in intensity from mild uneasiness to intense shock. The original conceptual framework incorporated this feature by considering it as an integral part of the problem-setting process. The results of data analysis and a reconsideration of the literature on purpose indicate that motivation to reflect deserves more particular attention. Thus, the second distinctive feature of the 'new' conceptual framework is the isolation of the impetus for reflection or for an 'act of reflection', as the new framework calls it. This latter change in terminology clarifies that the focus is on the individual instance rather than on reflection in general. Though the intent was there in the original framework, it was not clearly specified.

The results of this study suggest that the impetus to engage in an act of reflection requested by a teacher education program is influenced by the initial abilities and propensities of the preservice teacher. One of the distinctive qualities of Alert Novices seems to be the desire to know. Driven by their 'passionate creeds' and 'why' questions, they appear to be internally motivated to engage in both spontaneous and structured reflection, sometimes despite their own misgivings. The Common-sense Thinkers may not only be without these personal purposes, they may also have interfering attitudes, emotions and values. If, as many emotion theorists suggest, emotions not only influence motivation, they 'constitute the primary motivational system for human beings' (Izard, 1977, p. 3), an understanding of student teachers' emotional states and traits becomes critical to reflective teacher education.

Without the internal motivation to reflect, the Common-sense Thinkers may depend more upon the external motivation provided by the structural features of the task. But reflective teacher education is not confined to the encouragement of reflection in individual assignments. As Feiman-Nemser and Buchmann (1985) observe, one of the aims of reflective teacher education is to transform Common-sense Thinkers into Pedagogical Thinkers. Since Pedagogical Thinkers engage in reflection as a matter of course, assignments should also help Common-sense Thinkers to develop general and lasting intrinsic motivation. These student teachers need help in developing internal purposes for reflection which may include the adoption of a 'passionate creed' and learning to ask 'why' questions.

There is a second internal/external dimension to the impetus for reflection in preservice teacher education which was apparent in the various topics of reflection chosen by the participants. The source of a triggering perplexity is often the occurrence of an external environmental event which the person cannot control or does not understand. The purpose of the reflection is then to regain control of the situation or to better comprehend an issue. In contrast, the individual may simply be engaged in thinking about his or her own internal views, feelings, or experiences or, in fact, his or her own thinking processes, and, while doing so, encounter a standard, idea, or process he or she would like to attack more systematically. The purpose of this reflection is to enhance the understanding or functioning of internal cognitions and/or emotions. In either case, an emotional reaction or sudden intuition can also serve as an impetus to reflection.

The reflection asked for by teacher education programs is, by definition, externally motivated, and even for some Alert Novices, may remain so. The issue of how to engender internal motivation for an externally imposed endeavor is an important one, but particularly so for Common-sense Thinkers who do not seem to have the propensity for doing so in the first place.

The purpose frames the particular act of reflection which is carried out in a distinct context, in a certain way, on a specific topic. A third variation in the 'new' conceptual framework is a more direct incorporation and definitive treatment of the latter three aspects of reflective thinking. Most of the modifications in this section are more cosmetic than substantive. The first, 'condition', has been altered very little. The label was changed to 'context' only because the term seemed preferable; the underlying concept is the same. Since the listing of only artifacts and partner/observer was too limiting, I chose, instead, to use the broader notation 'structural aids to reflection'. Thus, research-like tasks, seminar discussions, and whatever else has been and will be developed can be included with artifacts and partner/observers. An implication of this research is that structural aids to reflection matter and, depending upon the details of their design and implementation, can affect the nature and quality of the outcomes of reflective acts. I also added other contextual features apparent in the literature — timing and location. Although the latter were not a focus for my particular studies, I believe them important to our understanding of reflection in teacher education and, therefore, a significant feature of the new model.

To carry out an act of reflection, a certain process must be employed. Particular procedures need to be followed in ways distinctive to reflective thinking. The original conceptual framework employed the three steps delineated by Dewey (1910): problem-setting, means/ends analysis, and generalization. Though noted from the outset that all steps were not necessary to each act of reflection, the numbers are eliminated in the new model to emphasize this point. Similarly, the attitudes of openmindedness, responsibility and wholeheartedness only implied in the former framework, are overtly included in the new one because of their centrality in my scoring criteria. The results of this study tend to support the potential of the conceptualization and the measurement tools deriving from it. Further study needs to be undertaken in which additional attention is devoted to if and how reflection differs from other types of thinking. Dewey seems to equate it with logical thinking and Hullfish and Smith (1961) with thinking itself. The 'new' conceptual framework implies some differences from thinking in general and logical thinking in particular that need to be investigated. The relationship between reflection and intuition should also be explored.

Dewey (1932) distinguishes reflection from intuition. He claims that intuitions are psychological and are indications of formed habit rather than thoughtful judgment. He does grant that intuitions may have been the result of prior reflectivity and that they can, in practice, be useful:

> The reaction of an expert in any field is, relatively at least, intuitive rather than reflective. . . . The results of prior experience, including previous conscious thinking, get taken up into direct habits, and express themselves in direct appraisals of value. Most of our moral judgments are intuitive, but this fact is not a proof of the existence of a separate faculty of moral insight, but is the result of past experience funded into direct outlook upon the scene of life (p. 124).

These intuitions have limitations, however. First, they may have been faulty from the outset if they were the result of misdirected education. Second, they may become too habitual and not subject to the re-evaluation and revision necessary for continual development and situational adaptation.

Goodman (1984) takes a different stance on intuition. He sees it not as distinct from, but as a part of, reflection. He describes three ways of thinking: routine, rational, and intuitive, and proposes that reflective thinking occurs with the integration of rational and intuitive thought processes. The teacher may have 'flashes of inspiration and creative insights, but it requires careful planning and rational decision-making to put novel ideas into practice' (p. 20). I suggest that these 'flashes of inspiration and creative insights' or 'intuitions' function within the framework as a potential impetus for reflection. They may operate similarly to 'felt difficulties' but in a more positive sense. I tend to agree with both Goodman and Dewey that intuitive thinking is not the same as reflective thinking and may operate separately. However, if intuitions are to have influence upon the views and practices of teachers, they should be subjected to, or included in, reflection as much as possible. As Shulman (1988) put it:

> To educate is to teach in a way that includes an account of why you do as you do. While tacit knowledge may be characteristic of many things that teachers do, our obligation as teacher educators must be to make the tacit explicit. Teachers will become better educators when they can begin to have explicit answers to the questions: 'How do I know what I know? How do I know the reasons for what I do? Why do I ask my students to perform or think in particular ways?' The capacity to answer such questions not only lies at the heart of what we mean by becoming skilled as a teacher; it also requires a combining of reflection on practical experience and reflection on theoretical understanding (p. 33).

The tacit assumptions, values and intuitions of teachers, particularly novice teachers, need to be surfaced and analyzed.

The content of reflection in general, according to this perspective, is both practical and theoretical. In any single act of reflection the content might be either or both. The reflective cases in this study seemed to exemplify the latter instance. That is, in the consideration of a practical problem, theoretical perspectives were brought to bear and subjected to their own analysis. Conversely, in the evaluation of a standard for judgment or an educational principle, the implications for practice were generated and explored. In Elliott's (1987) words: 'Practical deliberation integrates empirical with theoretical/philosophical inquiry' (p. 163). With this conceptualization, levels of reflection, like van Manen's (1977) become irrelevant. Such distinctions may create what Shulman (1988) objects to as a false dichotomy (or in this case, a 'tri-chotomy').

The topic of consideration can still vary within this framework and may include such categories as those Richert (1987) uses in her study: teacher, student, context, content, general pedagogy, content specific pedagogy, and personal. Regardless of topic, each act of reflection might well include practical/technical, social/political, and moral/ethical arguments and outcomes, but with varying intensities of focus according to purpose. Preservice teachers need to be encouraged to reflect on as many domains as possible, during the program and beyond, in ways that embrace both practical and theoretical content.

The results of reflection vary depending upon the purpose, the context, the content and the procedures actually followed. The primary outcome is a new comprehension(s). The final distinctive feature of the 'new' conceptual framework is its delineation of potential outcomes. These changes seemed to be called for by the previous changes in the model reflecting the results of data analysis. Particularly relevant were the depictions of Common-sense Thinkers and Alert Novices. Since one of the primary aims of reflection in teacher education is to move Common-sense Thinkers further along the continuum of pedagogical thinking (see Figure 2.2), then some of the desired outcomes should be changes in the features originally distinguishing them from Alert Novices. The categories listed under 'new comprehensions' thus represent the qualities included in the depictions of Common-sense Thinkers and Alert Novices in the first section of the model: a 'new comprehension' can be an improved ability to carry out an act of reflection; it may be an additional or changed belief about a particular topic in such areas as curriculum, subject matter, or instruction — pedagogical content knowledge; it can be an attitude or value about what is important to teach and why — a moral standard or theoretical assumption; and/or it may be an alteration of one's emotional states or traits.

Because reflection is a process involving judgment in indeterminate situations, the quality of the results will vary. But the outcomes may be strengthened or weakened by manipulation of the contributing features. At any rate, the new comprehensions should always be tentative and subject to continual revision. As such, reflection has a future-orientation: 'We cannot undo the past; we can affect the future' (Dewey, 1932, p. 170). Reflective teachers reflect in order to learn-to improve their understanding of, feelings about, and responses to the world of teaching. These new comprehensions may or may not actually serve to incite or inform solutions to current or future practical problems. Thus, the solving of practical problems is seen to be a secondary outcome of reflection.

Grimmett (1988) talks about three categories of conceptions of reflection: 1) reflection in order to direct or control practice; 2) reflection to inform practice by deliberating and choosing among competing versions of 'good teaching', and 3) reflection to appreciate or apprehend practice by reconstructing experience the end of which is a new possibility for action. As a result of the latter, the teacher may gain new understandings of action situations, self-as-teacher, or taken-for-granted assumptions about teaching. I propose that the first two are not separate conceptions, but can operate instead as spurs to reflection or as final results of the process. Alone they are more like habitual response or mechanical action. To qualify as reflection, the procedures of reflection and the resulting new comprehensions should intervene. As Greene (1986) put it:

> Those who are thoughtful, who want to be intelligent about what they are doing in the classroom, sometimes find simple pragmatic tests to validate what they are doing. Others, more philosophically inclined, recognize that practical judgments may best be made when, indeed, what they 'know and cherish' is brought to bear. This means engagement in a deliberate effort to relate what research has enabled them to understand about (say) learning behaviors at different stages, the interpretations and analyses they have been able to make with regard to the meanings of disparate terms, the diagnoses they have been able to make of the social realities in which they are enmeshed, the theories of education they have learned or devised, and the values and commitments that permeate their lives. All of this can provide only a partial, perspectival view; but to 'stop and think' may be all anyone can do (p. 481).

Perhaps reflection is the process engaged in by those 'more philosophically inclined'.

The 'new' definition of reflection in teacher education I have proposed is not revolutionary. As stated before, the literature on the topic is fairly substantial and the requisite 'pieces' seem already to have been formulated and explicated. The problem has been less an absence of definition, than a plethora of meanings with considerable variation. Furthermore, many of the treatments of the topic have been rather narrow in focus, dealing with only a piece of a larger process. My definition is the result of an effort to resolve conflicting perspectives, to examine what has been taken for granted, and to incorporate all relevant factors and associate them in explicit and meaningful ways. The result, I believe, is a comprehensive definition that can guide research and practice in reflective teacher education. It should allow us to engage in meaningful discussion on the issues and to produce more comparable results.

References

BOUD, D., KEOGH, R. and WALKER, D. (1985) 'Promoting reflection in learning', in BOUD, D., KEOGH, R. and WALKER, D. (eds) *Reflection: Turning experience into learning*, New York: Nichols Publishing Co.

CALDERHEAD, J. (1989) 'Reflective teaching and teacher education', *Teaching and Teacher Education*, **5**(1), pp. 43–51.

COPELAND, W.D. (1991) 'The reflective practitioner in teaching: Toward a research agenda'. Symposium proposal for the Annual Meeting of the American Educational Research Association, Chicago, IL.

DEWEY, J. (1910) *How we think*, Boston: D.C. Heath and Co., Publishers.

— (1932) *Theory of the moral life*, New York: Holt, Rinehart and Winston, Inc.

ELLIOTT, J. (1987) 'Teachers as researchers', in M.J. DUNKIN (ed.) *The International Encyclopedia of Teaching and Teacher Education*, Oxford, England: Pergamon Press.

FEIMAN-NEMSER, S. and BUCHMANN, M. (1985) *The first year of teacher preparation: Transition to pedagogical thinking?* Michigan State University: The Institute for Research on Teaching, Research Series No. 156.

FRIJDA, N.H. (1987) Comment on Oatley and JOHNSON-LAIRD's 'Towards a cognitive theory of emotions'. *Cognition and Emotion*, **1**(1), pp. 51–58.

GOODMAN, J. (1984) 'Reflection and teacher education: A case study and theoretical analysis', *Interchange*, **15**(3), pp. 9–26.

GREENE, M. (1986) 'Philosophy and teaching', in M.C. WITTROCK (ed.) *Handbook of research on teaching. Third Edition*, New York: Macmillan Publishing Co.

GRIMMETT, P.P. (1988) 'The nature of reflection and Schon's conception in perspective', in GRIMMETT, P.P. and ERICKSON, G.L. (eds) *Reflection in teacher education*, New York: Teachers College Press.

HULLFISH, H.G. and SMITH, P.G. (1961) *Reflective thinking: The method of education*, New York: Dodd, Mead and Company.

IZARD, C.E. (1977) *Human emotions*, New York: Plenum Press.

KITCHENER, K.S. (1983) 'Educational goals and reflective thinking', *The Educational Forum*, **48**(1), pp. 75–96.

— (1986) 'The reflective judgment model: Characteristics, evidence, and measurement', in R.A. MINES and K.S. KITCHENER (eds) *Adult cognitive development: Methods and models*, New York: Praeger Publishers.

LABOSKEY, V.K. (1989) 'An exploration of the nature and stability of reflectivity in preservice teachers', unpublished doctoral dissertation, Stanford University, Stanford, CA.

LEVENTHAL, H. and SCHERER, K. (1987) 'The relationship of emotion to cognition: A functional approach to a semantic controversy', *Cognition and Emotion*, **1**(1), pp. 3–28.

Vicki Kubler LaBoskey

OATLEY, K. and JOHNSON-LAIRD, P.N. (1987) 'Towards a cognitive theory of emotions', *Cognition and Emotion*, **1**(1), pp. 29–50.

RICHERT, A.E. (1987) 'Reflex to reflection: Facilitating reflection in novice teachers', Unpublished doctoral dissertation, Stanford University, Stanford, CA.

SHULMAN, L.S. (1986) 'Those who understand: Knowledge growth in teaching', *Educational Researcher*, 4–14.

— (1988) 'The dangers of dichotomous thinking in education', in GRIMMETT, P.P. and ERICKSON, G.L. (eds) *Reflection in teacher education*, New York: Teachers College Press.

VAN MANEN, M. (1977) 'Linking ways of knowing with ways of being practical', *Curriculum Inquiry*, **6**, pp. 205–228.

3 Theory, Theorizing and Reflection in Initial Teacher Education

Donald McIntyre

In the United Kingdom in recent years, 'theory' has been in danger of becoming a dirty word in relation to teacher education. The initiative in debate over the future of teacher education has been taken by right-wing populists such as O'Hear (1988), the Hillgate Group (1989), and Lawlor (1990) who have caricatured the kind of theory taught in teacher education programmes and have questioned the need for *any* theoretical content in these programmes. Practical competence in teaching is what is needed, they suggest, and such competence can best be acquired through practice in school-based training.

The extent to which such a remarkably primitive view of teacher education has dominated the attention of the news media, and has clearly won the sympathy of many in the media and in government, has been understandably frightening for serious teacher educators in this country. The challenge is, none the less, a useful one if it leads us to reconsider carefully our own beliefs in relation to the place we want to give to theory and the nature of that theory. This paper represents some initial attempts in that direction.

Theory and/or Theorizing?

Let us start by noting that it is not the populists' rejection of 'theory' as such that has most tended to disturb British teacher educators, but rather their lack of concern with the development of *reflective* and especially *critically reflective* teachers. Rudduck (1991) represents quite a widespread view, I believe, when she suggests that, in order to win allies in the fight to sustain teacher education programmes aimed at fostering reflective teachers, we might fruitfully abandon the use of the word 'theory'. It is, she implies, part of the baggage we have inherited from the past, not part of the core of what we need to fight for. More generally, paralleling the change in emphasis in primary and secondary schools from content to process, there has in the last decade been a notable shift in the expressed concerns of British teacher educators — I cannot comment on their practice — from the theoretical *content* which student teachers should understand to the intellectual *processes* in which student teachers should learn to engage.

Alexander (1984) was one of the first to describe this change in emphasis. He described an evolution in thinking about the theoretical basis for learning to teach through seven stages from an early 'eclectic mixture of psychology, 'great educators' and classroom prescription' (p. 143), through various versions of 'given' theory which sought to inform practice, as with an applied science, then a notion of codifying the craft knowledge of experienced teachers (McNamara and Desforges, 1978), and eventually a view:

> that the task for teacher educators was to concentrate less on what the student should know, more on how he might think. The core of this further alternative was a notion of theory as intellectual process rather than as propositional knowledge: 'theorizing' (Alexander, 1986, p. 145).

This view of 'theory as process' was described by Alexander in 1984 as a 'possibility' which had been articulated 'rather than an actuality'. Since then, however, such a view has seemed to inform an increasing number of British teacher education courses. This British scene, in which 'theorizing', 'theory as process', or 'reflecting' has increasingly been seen as an attractive *alternative* in initial teacher education to a conception of theory as propositional knowledge, seems to be rather different from the North American scene. Linda Valli (1993), in her illuminating account of reflective teacher education programmes in the United States, comments on the irony of the concurrent problematizing of the theory/practice relation in such programmes and the investment at the same time in attempts to articulate clearly and fully an *academic knowledge base* on which teaching is seen to depend. There is no such irony apparent in this country. An authoritative compendium entitled *Knowledge Base for the Beginning Teacher*, such as that published by the American Association of Colleges for Teacher Education (Reynolds, 1989), would I think be very much at odds with the climate of the times here. Wheras there is an increasing emphasis on the processes of theorizing, reflecting and questioning on both sides of the Atlantic, in North America this seems to me to complement a confidence that there is a large body of academic knowledge about teaching and schooling which the beginning teacher can valuably learn, even if questioning the validity or relevance of that knowledge is also important. Even the seminal paper by Zeichner and Liston (1987) on 'Teaching Student Teachers to Reflect' describes a course which follows on from, rather than replaces, a large number of other courses with substantial and wide-ranging theoretical content. The confidence that there are substantial bodies of theoretical content knowledge which student teachers ought to learn seems to me to be absent on this side of the Atlantic.

Given this state of affairs, I can as a first step reformulate my problem (about what place to give to what kind of theory) in terms of a question about the adequacy of replacing theory as propositional knowledge by a concern for theorizing, or perhaps for reflection, in initial teacher education.

As it happened, Alexander very generously exemplified the idea of theory as process in teacher education by reference to some ideas of my own (McIntyre, 1980); so perhaps I ought, if I am consistent, to welcome the replacement of theory as content by theory as process. Alexander accurately described my conception of learning to teach as:

> a continual process of hypothesis-testing framed by detailed analysis of the values and practical constraints fundamental to teaching. The 'theory' for teacher education should therefore incorporate (i) speculative theory, (ii) the findings of empirical research, (iii) the craft knowledge of practising teachers; but none should be presented as having prescriptive implications for practice: instead students should be encouraged to approach their own practice with the intention of testing hypothetical principles drawn from the consideration of these different types of knowledge (Alexander, *op. cit.*, p. 146).

Alexander also accurately described this view as Popperian; and that is very helpful, because it demonstrates why I cannot agree with him that we are talking about a replacement of theory as content by theory as process. For Popper, all scientific knowledge is tentative, awaiting falsification and rejection or refinement: the process is central to the nature of scientific knowledge. That, however, does not mean that our existing scientific knowledge is trivial, arbitrary or lacking in practical value. On the contrary, we use our scientific knowledge for practical purposes while we wait for, or arrange for, its falsification. Similarly, I would argue, the theoretical knowledge which we offer student teachers should be treated by them as tentative, inadequate and constantly to be questioned and, where appropriate, falsified; but it should also be knowledge which we offer them because we believe it to be of practical value to them as teachers. Our commitment to the process of experimentation and falsification should be equalled by our commitment to making available to our students theoretical knowledge which they will mostly, with refinement, be able usefully to assimilate to their professional thinking. So acceptance of the importance of theory as process need not, and should not in my view, limit the importance we attach to theory as content. I shall return later to the issue of *what* theoretical knowledge is likely to be useful for student teachers; but first there are issues about reflecting and theorizing which require consideration.

Institutionalizing the Process of Theorizing

The view of theorizing which I had outlined earlier became, in the last few years, one of the basic elements of the so-called Internship scheme for the initial professional education of secondary school teachers at Oxford; and it is through its institutionalization in that context that we have been able to reflect on it. Very briefly, the core of the scheme in this respect involves student teachers being attached in pairs to subject teachers called mentors in whose schools they spend part or all of their time each week throughout the year from October until June. Their whole classroom-related curriculum, university-based and school-based, is planned jointly by the mentors and the curriculum tutors for each subject area. They agree on what issues should be considered in the curriculum, when these issues should be considered, and what activities will be appropriate for the student teachers in the school and in the university in relation to these issues. It is an explicit principle that different kinds of relevant knowledge, but equally important kinds of know-ledge, should be accessed from university and school sources. Crucially, it is also an explicit principle that no knowledge, whatever the nature or source, should be assumed to be valid, but should instead be questioned in relation to a range of criteria. Very importantly, indeed centrally, that applies to all ideas important to individual student teachers, not just to those they have learned from their tutors or mentors. It is expected that university tutors will generally find themselves best equipped to help student teachers to ex-amine ideas or practices in terms of their conceptual clarity and coherence, in terms of the educational and social values they imply, in terms of the generalizability of their viability and effectiveness, and in terms of their longer-term contribution to children's learning. It is expected that mentors will generally find themselves best equipped to help student teachers to examine ideas or practices in terms of the equally important criteria of their acceptability, viability and effectiveness in context and of their adequacy as a guide to practice. No consensus on any issue is assumed.

I do not want to pretend that that, in all its aspects, is what routinely happens at Oxford; but it happens sufficiently often and sufficiently fully for us to be able to say that it is a practicable set of ideas and a powerfully effec-tive set of practices when they are put into operation.

In the remainder of this paper, I want to use our experience at Oxford as a background against which issues about 'reflection', 'theorizing' and 'theory' in initial teacher education can be examined.

Reflection as Means or Goal in Initial Teacher Education

Reflection, as Calderhead (1989) has very clearly established, is a term used in a wide variety of ways. It is therefore useful to define the term as it is used here. Following Lucas (1991), reflection is defined as 'systematic enquiry into one's own practice to improve that practice and to deepen one's understanding of it'. While that is quite a broad definition, it usefully identifies 'reflection' as a sub-category of 'theorizing' in general. In considering the nature and importance of reflection, so defined, in teacher education programmes, it is necessary to differentiate clearly between reflection as something which teachers should learn to do competently (a goal) and reflection as a means to the attainment of that or other goals.

It seems to me necessary in the first instance to argue that reflection is a much more central means of learning for experienced practitioners, than it can or need be for novices. There are at least three reasons for this. First, so much of experienced teachers' practice is automated or intuitive, dependent on understandings that are not usually articulated, that learning for them is dependent on bringing to consciousness and examining the assumptions and considerations which make sense of their actions as teachers; without reflection, they cannot change their practice in a controlled or deliberate way. For novices, on the other hand, almost every halting step that they take needs conscious deliberation and planning: their competence, such as it is, is achieved through conscious control; they do not need to reflect in order to be conscious of what they have been trying to do and know. This does not mean that they bring no unexamined assumptions to their teaching, or that they do not depend on taken-for-granted analogies with previous experiences in other contexts, but simply that such assumptions and analogies are not embedded in fluent, well-learned classroom practices: they do not have to be unravelled or unlearned as established aspects of classroom expertise. Instead, the beginning teacher is much more able to learn through deliberating about the nature of the expertise that he or she *wants* to develop.

Second, experienced teachers are *able* to learn much more through reflection on their experience. Like Schön's expert practitioners (Schön, 1983), they have extensive repertoires of past experiences on which they can draw in order to illuminate current problems; and, when they use the possibilities of constructing new frames by modifying and combining old ones, they have very rich, even although bounded, capacities for thinking creatively through reflection in and on their experience. None of this is true for the novice. For the novice who needs to develop ways of construing situations and possibilities for effective action within these situations, there is a necessary dependence on ideas from sources outside his or her own teaching experiences. These *may* be their experiences in other kinds of context, but more usefully in most cases they will be ideas gained from working with experienced teachers, from tutors or from reading; and, being ideas which are not rooted in their own experience, they will tend initially to be used less fluently and less flexibly.

Third, at a time in their career when they need, and are well placed to use, ideas from others, student teachers can more easily gain access to these ideas than they are likely to be able to at other stages in their careers. Certainly it is through reflection on their own teaching that novices can be helped to see the need for ideas from other sources; and certainly they will not readily or quickly abandon their preconceptions. My argument is, however, that in extreme contrast to the needs of experienced practitioners, the needs of novices and the best opportunities available to them are in gaining access to useful ideas from various other sources, with reflection on their own experience being primarily useful to them for the important but limited purpose of motivating and enabling them to see the need for these ideas from external sources. I think this is a very obvious point, but I am conscious that in making it I am disagreeing if not with Schön himself at least with some enthusiasts for his ideas (e.g. Furlong *et al.*, 1988). On the other hand, although reflection has only a limited importance as a *means* to learning for the student teacher, learning to reflect must surely be an important *goal* for student-teachers, since it is through reflection on their own teaching that they will increasingly with experience be able to continue learning.

Thus, in initial teacher education, reflection on one's own practice has, it is suggested, two main functions. The first of these is the development of student teachers' immediate understanding of their own problems and needs, in order to give direction and purpose to their search for helpful ideas from other sources and their theorizing about these ideas. The second, the benefits of which are long-term, is guided *practice* in the skills and habits of reflection, skills and habits which will be increasingly valuable, and on which they as teachers will be increasingly dependent, as they become more experienced practitioners.

Different Levels of Theorizing and Reflecting

I want now to discuss in relation to our Oxford programme three different kinds or levels of theorizing and reflecting about which there seems to be a growing consensus. The three levels are differentiated in terms of the comprehensiveness of what is considered problematic in educational practice. Zeichner and Liston (1987) note a convergence between the thinking of van Manen (1977) and Tom (1984) in distinguishing these levels, and it is not difficult to see a close connection also with distinctions made by critical theorists such as Carr and Kemmis (1986). At the first or *technical* level, the concern is with the effective attainment of given goals. At the second or *practical* level, the concern is with the assumptions, predispositions, values and consequences with which actions are linked. At the third, *critical* or *emancipatory* level, the concern includes wider ethical, social and political issues, including crucially the institutional and societal forces which may constrain the individual's freedom of action or limit the efficacy of his or her actions. The primary concerns of three different elements of the Oxford programme are respectively with these three levels of reflectivity.

In relation to student teachers' own classroom teaching, the year is divided into two phases, the primary concerns of which respectively correspond roughly to the first two levels of reflectivity. For the first phase, a list of consensual criteria are specified in terms of short-term goals which student teachers are told they have to learn to be able to attain — achieving and maintaining classroom order and purposeful activity, gaining pupils' attention and interest, ensuring that pupils know what they are expected to do, that they understand the content of lessons, etc. These criteria correspond quite clearly to the broadly-defined 'efficacy' criteria which Anne Proctor (1993) describes as supervisors' priority concerns. These criteria represent the standards of classroom competence which tutors and mentors agree are minimally necessary for student teachers to qualify as teachers. They leave open, it will be noted, the *means* by which the short-term goals are to be attained; these will depend on the specific contexts, and may also depend on the personal skills and commitments of the individual student teacher. During this first phase, it is the student teacher's primary task to reflect on his or her teaching, and to learn from other sources, so as to become able consistently to meet these criteria. The *reflection* is thus primarily at the technical level, although in developing a repertoire of skills, the student teacher's success is likely to depend both on deliberate use of ideas from a wide variety of sources, and also on *theorizing* about these ideas in relation to a wide range of criteria including some at the practical and critical levels.

After completing Phase 1 satisfactorily, the student teachers are asked to concentrate on learning to evaluate and to develop their own teaching. Here the concern is with their ability to articulate and justify their own criteria for evaluating self-selected aspects of their teaching, to use these criteria through collecting and interpreting appropriate evidence, and to explore useful ways of developing their teaching in the light of these self-evaluations. This then is concerned with *practical* reflectivity, where the emphasis is on articulating one's own criteria and in evaluating and developing one's own practice. We see this phase as the one in which the central goal is for student teachers to learn habits and skills of reflecting. In order to do so, however, student teachers need to engage in extensive wider theorizing, about, for example, the nature of their subjects, their students' longer-term learning processes and the wider purposes of schooling.

We find it necessary to distinguish these two phases for three main reasons. First, mentors would, we believe, be properly impatient with an emphasis on student teachers exploring the implications for classroom practice of their own educational values before they had attained a minimal classroom competence. Second, most student teachers themselves lack the concern or the confidence to work through the implications of their ideals until they have first assured themselves that, in the eyes of their mentors and tutors they are 'all right', competent, 'can do the job'. Third, it takes two-thirds of the year before most student teachers have learned enough about the complexities of classroom teaching to be able meaningfully to attempt to relate their classroom practice to their educational values.

What about the third, *critical* or *emancipatory*, level of reflectivity? It is certainly of fundamental importance that beginning teachers should learn to see how their efforts as teachers, and the effects of their efforts, are shaped by the institutional and societal structures within which they work, and by the ideologies which support these structures. In particular, it is important that they should understand how their own work, shaped by these structures and ideologies, can serve interests different from, and sometimes in conflict with, those of the pupils whom they are teaching; and that they should be helped to begin to search for strategies through which, individually and corporately, they can contest the processes and the ideologies of schooling. But is reflection on their own practice the right place to start?

At the 1990 conference of the American Educational Research Association, in a symposium on Action Research in Teacher Education (Stevenson and Noffke, 1990), three papers described specific teacher education programmes based on action research, all of them, it seemed to me, carefully planned, theoretically informed and sensitively implemented, from Deakin, Wisconsin and Buffalo Universities. All of them were able to report substantial success. What was striking, however, was that in all three cases, the investigators expressed disappointment at their lack of success in attaining their most treasured goal, that of reflection by their students at the critical or emancipatory level. The student teachers or teachers had in all three cases been generally thoughtful in interpreting their own teaching, its implicit values and its effects; but they had systematically failed to use their action research as a basis for looking critically, as they had been encouraged to do, at the institutional or societal context of their teaching. In another excellent study, which may be quoted as an extreme case, primary school teachers in black South African schools whom Melanie Walker helped to engage in action research on their teaching of reading were eager to explore the effects of their teaching and to develop their classroom practice; but even in their appalling conditions, they were quite unready to use their own teaching as a starting point for considering how social, political and economic factors were limiting the value of their work (Walker, 1991).

Judging from these cases, it does not seem that teachers or student teachers are led, through reflecting on their own practice, and especially through action research on it, to take a critical view of the structural or ideological context in which they are working. Nor, I think, should that surprise us: reflecting on one's own practice, and especially engaging in action research, leads one to emphasize one's own agency; and if things go wrong, the logic of the study leads one to explore alternatives for one's own action, not explanations from quite different directions. Of course if one has already developed a theoretical understanding of the situation in terms of external or ideological factors, and is therefore viewing one's actions and their effects in relation to a theorized context, then one is better placed to engage in a more far-reaching analysis.

In Oxford, therefore, student teachers' study of the social and institutional context of teaching is not based upon their reflection on their own teaching but instead is aimed to feed into that reflection. In a programme parallel to that concerned with classroom teaching, theoretical studies of such matters as 'special needs', social class, race, gender, assessment, education and industry, and environmental education are related to investigation of the practices and policies of the school in which each group of about ten student teachers is placed. Tensions between practices found in the schools and the abstract analyses and theoretical ideals studied at university and in the literature are deliberately exploited so that both theory and practice can be critically examined. It is thus through theorizing about others' practices that student teachers are helped to gain a critical perspective on the contexts within which they are working; and it is on the basis of such an understanding that they are encouraged to introduce this level of reflectivity into their reflection on their own practices.

Finally, in relation to process, I would re-emphasize the limited role of reflection in initial teacher education. Even in relation to the three levels of reflectivity discussed here, it seems clear that reflection, although important as an element in learning, is important either as a subsidiary element to other kinds of learning and theorizing or as a goal to be attained, a kind of learning to be practised and developed for future use. In addition, however, we should surely expect much more theorizing to be done during initial teacher education which is *not* connected to student teachers' reflection on their individual practices. There is much to be read, to be discussed, and to be found in the practice of experienced teachers which merits examination and mental trial but which it will not be possible for the individual student teacher to test in his or her own practice, because of constraints of time, opportunity or expertise. Reflection concerns one's present practices, but theorizing concerns the whole world of possibilities for the future.

Theoretical Content for Initial Teacher Education

In order to theorize fruitfully, student teachers need appropriate content about which they can theorize. What kind of content should that be?

Three preliminary comments are necessary. First, there is a very large amount of theoretical knowledge about education which beginning teachers could usefully learn. Understanding of, for example, the historical, social and organizational contexts in which they work, the processes through which children learn, the social interaction processes which can occur in classrooms, the ways in which political, economic and cultural factors influence the outcomes of schooling, different philosophical conceptions of education or the different approaches to schooling adopted in different countries, cannot but enrich the thoughtfulness and intelligence with which teachers approach their work. Furthermore, there are in all these areas extensive and coherent bodies of soundly-based theoretical knowledge which can be made accessible to students. The problem, it is abundantly clear, is not one of finding valuable theoretical knowledge for student teachers to learn. It is rather a problem of deciding what knowledge it is most necessary for them to learn in the limited amount of time made available for their initial professional education.

The second necessary preliminary comment concerns a distinction between teacher educators' long-term aspirations and their immediate plans. Because the systematic study of teaching is at a very early stage, it is necessary that teacher educators' own research and theorizing should be guided by visions of the kind of theoretical knowledge that could valuably be developed about teaching and subsequently used in teacher education programmes. Thus McNamara and Desforges' (1978) aspiration to investigate and codify teachers' craft knowledge, so that it could be used in initial teacher education, remains potentially viable and valuable. Similarly Hirst's (1990) aspiration that student-teachers' professional education should: 'in both the theoretical and practical parts of the course', lead them to 'see themselves as part of a professional group working towards an ever increasing consensus about practice' (p. 153) may be attractive and even plausible, but the necessary identification of a consensual body of 'practical principles' is a task still to be undertaken. Or again, Elliott (1991), outlining a 'practical science view of teacher education', suggests that:

> the primary research role of schools of education is to collaborate with educational practitioners in reflecting about the range and variety of practical situations they encounter as educators. ... Its main aim would be to develop and maintain the stock of professional knowledge. ... Such outcomes would themselves constitute a major part of the teaching resources within schools of education (pp. 23–24).

It is essential that teacher educators should develop such visions and formulate such enterprises; but the practicability of their visions of teacher education depends, even in the future, upon how successful their uncertain research enterprises prove to be. In the meantime, we need to plan teacher education programmes which are viable in our present state of knowledge; and it is with this latter purpose that this paper is concerned.

The third necessary preliminary comment concerns the difficult distinction between theoretical and practical knowledge. Practical knowledge is viewed here as that knowledge which is used to guide practice and to make sense of the particular situations in which one practices, but which is not articulated in terms which go beyond the particular. Theoretical knowledge, in contrast, is knowledge formulated in such a way as to imply claims to some kind of generalized validity. Here we are concerned only with the kinds of theoretical knowledge which one might plan for inclusion in a teacher education curriculum, not with the equally important theorizing that is derived from student teachers' experiences of their own and others' practices.

What kinds of theoretical knowledge is it most essential for student teachers to have access to within the constraints of, for example, a one-year course of initial professional education? I would argue that the core of the theoretical knowledge should be *suggestions for practice* in relation to the work which student teachers will subsequently be asked to undertake as teachers. These suggestions for practice should be selected for attention either because they are highly valued or because they are widely implemented or recommended. The main tasks of teacher education courses should be to understand, to theorize about, and most especially to evaluate the various suggestions for practice.

Three main arguments can be offered for this approach:

1) There is ample evidence of student teachers' general incapacity and/or unwillingness to make significant use of theoretical knowledge formulated in terms of interpretations or explanations of educational phenomena rather than in terms of suggestions for practice. This is most obviously true when that knowledge is organized in terms of 'foundation disciplines' such as psychology and sociology, but is also true for such knowledge when it is organized in terms of 'topics' or 'issues'. In view of the difficulty which expert lecturers have in making clear the implications for practice of such theoretical knowledge, it is unsurprising that student teachers should rarely attempt the task successfully.

    If the focus of concern is, in contrast, on suggestions for what teachers might appropriately do, then analytic and explanatory theory can be drawn upon where relevant to help student teachers to evaluate these suggestions. Within the limits of the time available this will generally mean that such theory will have to be predigested and made easily accessible.

    In brief then, this is simply the most effective way to make available to student teachers the most helpful ideas for them which can be derived from theoretical and research work in education.

2) A second argument for this approach is that, while providing student teachers with specific helpful ideas, it also introduces them to a kind of disciplined theorizing about practice which will continue to be of value to them during their professional lives. In the course of the year, the disciplines of such theorizing can be explained, modelled by tutors in relation to diverse ideas and aspects of practice, and regularly practised with guidance and feedback.

3) Thirdly, any real hope of effective integration of theory and practice, of higher education and school contributions to initial professional education, depends on having a core curriculum which satisfies both tutors and practising teachers and to which both groups are confident that they can contribute. This can be achieved

only where such a curriculum has been seriously and effectively negotiated; and such negotiation is greatly facilitated if it is first understood that the curriculum is to be focused on suggested practices for those tasks of teaching which are agreed to be most important. The difficulties of achieving shared ownership of an integrated curriculum should not be underestimated; and the terms in which that curriculum is formulated can be of critical importance in determining whether or not such shared ownership is genuinely achieved.

There seems little merit in attempting to categorize the different kinds of theory or other sources from which suggestions for practice are derived, or the different kinds of theory to be drawn upon in evaluating these suggestions. There are indeed many different kinds of theory to be drawn upon, including the reflections of experienced practitioners, generalized descriptions of what is judged to be good practice, ideas derived from social science theories, from philosophical positions or from technological possibilities, and the conclusions of many different kinds of educational research; but which of these are available and helpful tends to vary considerably according to the aspect of practice under discussion. Eclecticism and flexibility seem most important in deciding what can fruitfully be used.

It does seem important, however, to be explicit about the main disciplines which should inform theorizing about suggestions for practice. There are perhaps two main disciplines for student teachers to learn, which involve the application of 'theoretical' criteria. First there is *conceptual analysis*, crucial in relation to educational discourse, concerned with elucidating the meaning and questioning the meaningfulness of concepts and assertions, with identifying the hidden assumptions on which arguments depend, and with explicating the value-judgments implicit in arguments. Second, there is the *use of theory developed from empirical research*. Such theory may be relevant to a suggested practice in any of a wide variety of ways such as the effectiveness of the practice for achieving short-term or long-term goals, conditions upon which its use or its effectiveness depends, or implications of using it. Student teachers need to develop some ability to evaluate the adequacy with which theoretical claims are supported by research, and also to examine critically arguments linking theoretical claims to suggested practices. In this, however, student teachers (and teachers) are heavily dependent on the adequacy with which their tutors (and published texts) are able to synthesize available evidence and theory so as to make accessible both the grounds on which claims are made and problems with the quality of these grounds.

Equally important but very different kinds of discipline inform more 'practical' theorizing, concerned with the appropriateness of suggested practices for particular situations. All these disciplines of theorizing should be included *as explicit theoretical content* at early stages within teacher education courses: it is important that student teachers should understand the nature and rationale of the disciplines which should shape their theorizing.

More generally, if the limited time available for initial teacher education is to be used effectively, it is important that student teachers should understand, and where possible be persuaded of, the rationale for the activities in which they are asked to engage. Their programmes are, or certainly should be, designed in the light of substantial research-based knowledge about teachers' thinking and practice and the nature of teachers' expertise, and also about the processes by which people learn to teach. But student teachers themselves begin their courses with their own diverse preconceptions of what teaching involves and how it can best be learned; and only limited success is likely if student teachers' efforts are based on preconceptions inconsistent with the premises on which their courses are designed.

An important element in the theoretical content of teacher education courses should therefore be *suggestions for practice in learning how to teach*; and the evaluation of these practices should be a correspondingly important set of tasks, especially early in courses. Both the practices built into the planned programme and alternatives suggested by student teachers should be evaluated, mainly through discussion of research-based knowledge about teachers' thinking, classroom practice and learning. As for other learners, student teachers are likely to learn much more effectively if they have a shared understanding with their teachers about the nature of the knowledge which it will be useful to develop and about the means by which it may best be developed.

References

ALEXANDER, R.J. (1984) 'Innovation and continuity in the initial teacher education curriculum', in ALEXANDER, R.J., CRAFT, M. and LYNCH, J. (eds) *Change in Teacher Education: Context and provision since Robbins*, London: Holt, Rinehart and Winston, pp. 103–60.

CALDERHEAD, J. (1989) 'Reflective teaching and teacher education', *Teaching and Teacher Education*, **5**(1), pp. 43–51.

CARR, W. and KEMMIS, S. (1986) *Becoming Critical: Education, Knowledge and Action Research*, London: The Falmer Press.

ELLIOTT, J. (1991) 'Three perspectives on coherence and continuity in teacher education', paper prepared for UCET Annual Conference, November, University of East Anglia.

FURLONG, V.J., HIRST, P.H., POCKLINGTON, K. and MILES, S. (1988) *Initial Teacher Training and the Role of the School*, Milton Keynes: Open University Press.

HILLGATE GROUP (1989) *Learning to Teach*, London: Claridge Press in association with the Educational Research Centre.

HIRST, P.H. (1990) 'Internship: A View from Outside', in BENTON, P. (ed.), *The Oxfordshire Internship Scheme: Integration and Partnership in Initial Teacher Education*, London: Gulbenkian, pp. 147–160.

Donald McIntyre

LAWLOR, S. (1990) *Teachers mistaught: training in theories or education in subjects?* London: Centre for Policy Studies.

LUCAS, P. (1991) 'Reflection, New Practices and the Need for Flexibility in Supervising Student-Teachers', *Journal of Further and Higher Education*, **15**(2), pp. 84–93.

McINTYRE, D. (1980) 'The contribution of research to quality in teacher education' in HOYLE, E. and MEGARRY, J. (eds) *World Yearbook of Education 1980: Professional Development of Teachers*, London: Kogan Page, pp. 293–307.

McNAMARA, D. and DESFORGES, C. (1978) 'The social sciences, teacher education and the objectification of craft knowledge', *British Journal of Teacher Education*, **4**(1), pp. 17–36.

O'HEAR, A. (1988) *Who Teaches the Teachers?* London: Social Affairs Unit.

PROCTOR, K.A. (1993) 'Tutors' professional knowledge of supervision and the implications for supervision practice' (in this volume).

REYNOLDS, M. (ed.) (1989) *Knowledge Base for the Beginning Teacher*, Oxford: Pergamon Press for the American Association of Colleges for Teacher Education.

RUDDUCK, J. (1991) 'The Landscape of Consciousness and the Landscape of Action: Tensions in Teacher Education', *British Educational Research Journal*, **17**(4).

SCHÖN, D. (1983) *The Reflective Practitioner*, London: Temple Smith.

STEVENSON, R.B. and NOFFKE, S.E. (eds) (1990) *Action Research and Teacher Education: International Perspectives*, Buffalo Research Institute on Education for Teaching.

TOM, A.R. (1984) *Teaching as a Moral Craft*, New York, Longman.

VALLI, L. (1993) 'Reflective Teacher Education Programmes: an analysis of case studies' (in this volume).

VAN MANEN, (1977) 'Linking ways of knowing with ways of being practical', *Curriculum Inquiry*, **6**, pp. 205–228.

WALKER, M.J. (1991) 'Reflective Practitioners: A Case Study in Facilitating Teacher Development in Four African Primary Schools in Cape Town', Ph.D. Thesis, Faculty of Education, University of Cape Town.

ZEICHNER, K.M. and LISTON, D.P. (1987) 'Teaching student-teachers to reflect', *Harvard Educational Review*, **57**(1), pp. 23–48.

4   Eliciting Student Teachers' Personal Theories

Sarah Tann

This chapter is based on an analysis of the experience of thirty-two first-year primary B.Ed. students during a brief serial practice in their summer term. The students were required to work in groups of four and collaboratively to plan, teach and evaluate a sequence of lessons for the duration of a morning (9–12 a.m.) in each of four weekly visits. The planned sessions were for mixed-ability classes of approximately thirty pupils of either an infant class (6–7 year olds) or junior class (8–9 year olds). The students mostly worked with the same group of approximately four to five children, although each one took turns in addressing the whole class, for example in giving the initial introduction, handling a period of exploratory class discussion or final report back, reading a story or leading some singing. The sessions were cross-curricula in nature and were presented as part of an integrated 'topic' loosely focused on the concepts of health and safety. The students' group planning sessions were recorded but the main source of data was from the files which students were required to keep. These included the session plan (aims, objectives, methods, resources and rationale for each) and an evaluation of each session (what the students' learnt, what the children learnt, and what they planned next and why). The students were encouraged to evaluate their own group work skills in planning, as well as their own skills in group teaching and how the children worked in groups.

The classroom experience and the file assignment resulted in many discussions between students and staff concerning 'what is a reflective practitioner and why is the course based on this notion', 'what is personal theory and why is it important', 'what is a reflective file, what would it look like, and what could be learnt from it'. The initial answers to these questions will comprise the background context for this chapter, followed by an analysis of the files and their implications.

Background Context

What Conception of the 'Reflective Practitioner' Underpins the Course and Why?

The perennial concern with teacher education recurrently leads educationalists to argue for alternative approaches to the preparation of teaching and for variable conceptions of the role of teachers. Since the beginning of this century, Dewey (1916) argued that teachers needed to see themselves as more than classroom 'technicians' and should move beyond the goal of 'technical rationality' towards being a 'reflective teacher'. He identified a key distinction as being whether the teacher acts predominantly on the basis of 'routine action' or 'reflective action' — where reflective action 'entails active and persistent consideration of any belief or supposed form of knowledge in the light of the grounds that support it and the consequences to which it leads' [and] 'It is not the thing done but the quality of mind that goes into the doing which settles what is utilitarian and what is creative' (1933, p. 215).

This highlights a crucial debate concerning the expected role of a teacher. It is necessary to clarify the assumptions concerning 'teaching' before any reasoned start can be made in the debate on how students should be prepared for the teaching profession. For instance, if the teacher's role is considered to be to 'deliver a given curriculum' then certain consequences flow from this in terms of the knowledge, skills and attitudes best suited to such a (technician) task. If, however, the teacher's role is considered to be to 'diagnose learner needs, design cycles of learning, and contribute to educational decision-making (at classroom/school/political levels)' then a very different kind of preparation is needed which might be supported by a more critical and reflective approach. Research into the worlds of professionals suggests that they are characterized by complexity, uncertainty, instability, uniqueness and value conflict (Arkoff, 1979). If this is so, it could be argued that even to achieve the goal of curriculum deliverer, such a person would need to be able to think and act in an agile, analytic and reflective manner.

Dewey's distinction is the basis of that drawn by Schön (1983, 1987) when he refers to the need to move away from the 'scientific application' model of teacher training to that of the 'reflective practitioner'. Carr and Kemmis's (1986) model of teaching takes this one stage further and emphasizes the 'critical pedagogic thinking' needed to challenge educational assumptions, practices and outcomes not just within the classroom but also beyond those immediate concerns at institutional and societal levels.

In the last decade of this century the role of the teacher, and therefore the nature of training, is still being fundamentally questioned. Other professions in England and Wales, such as nursing and the police, as well as the teaching profession in other European countries, are all moving towards raising professional standards through extended training and incorporating 'reflection' in many different forms. However, in England and Wales political changes are forcing a reduction in training and encouraging an intensively school-based apprenticeship model.

For the purposes of this article, the discussion is situated within the critical and reflective framework and it is against that background that the concerns about eliciting personal theory will be presented. Further elaboration of the components of 'reflection' will be given below as they emerged from the students' negotiation of this concept.

What is Personal Theory and Why is it Considered Important?

One of the concerns regarding teacher education is that research studies have consistently shown that, regardless of the underlying conception of teaching or the philosophy of the course, teacher education programmes are a 'low impact-enterprise' (see Zeichner and Grant, 1981). Many different possible reasons have been offered to try to explain why such programmes have such little effect in encouraging students to challenge their previous assumptions or to examine critically the professional practice which they see around them. Zeichner *et al.* (1987) suggest factors which students experience before they begin a course and by which they may be heavily influenced, each of which undermine the impact any course might have. These include the powerful effect of the student's childhood heritage as a learner and the quality of the relationships experienced in educational contexts. These life-time experiences of the function and structure of education are likely to have contributed towards a definite conception of teaching roles and relationships to which the students cling. Further, students will have internalized teaching models which they observe before and during their training (both in school and on campus).

It is against this background that we need to view the growing interest in 'personal theory'. Johnson (1988) argues that teachers' pre-existing views of teaching and learning are so pervasive that unless directly challenged any attempt to alter teaching styles is ineffectual. Further, Ely (1991) believes that 'by recognizing and acknowledging our own myths and prejudices we can more effectively put them in their place. . . . Greater self-knowledge can help us to separate our thoughts and feelings from those of others, to be less judgmental, to appreciate others' experiences and thus to go beyond our own understandings and to develop professionally' (p. 122). Unless we engage students at a personal level they cannot make sense of the programme content: it does not connect.

It is important, however, to be clear as to what is meant by 'personal theory' and why such theories are believed to be significant. It is as well to remember that 'theory', in this professional context, refers to a person's set of beliefs, values, understandings, assumptions — the ways of thinking about the teaching profession. 'Personal theory' usually exists at an implicit level and may therefore be difficult to articulate and identify and hence difficult to unearth and examine. Such 'theories' are at a 'common sense' level and relate to types of life-experience based on knowledge and understandings that a person draws upon to guide action (Calderhead, 1987). If it is assumed that beliefs underpin action, then beliefs are clearly an important means to understanding how and why people act the way they do. Equally, that assumption itself needs to be examined and the occasions when beliefs are in conflict with action need also to be investigated. Further, it may be necessary to recognize that any individual is likely to have a series of theories, which will probably be incoherent and contradictory (Zeichner *et al.*, 1987). Individuals are often not aware of their own theories, nor that there are alternatives, until such time as they are overtly challenged. Berliner (1987) suggests that it is not only the content, origins and structure of our theories which are important, but also the ways in which they are held, the ease of access and linkage, and how theories are used which are critical.

By encouraging students to elicit and articulate their personal theories it allows access to their ways of conceptualizing teaching, learning and the curriculum. Goodman (1984) argues that we need to engage with these personal theories so that students can be aware of their own interpretive frameworks and be able to contrast theirs with both their peers and colleagues as well as with those educationalists who offer their personal theories publicly through publication or lecturing. In this way it may be possible to encourage students to 'connect' with alternative theories, to juxtapose personal and public theory and expand or clarify their own through the challenge of comparison and contrast and thus to overcome the 'limitations of experience' (Zeichner and Liston, 1987). This process enables them to articulate and then examine their common-sense hunches, so they can engage in theorizing by identifying their rationale, making their reasoning explicit, exploring alternatives through problematizing and hypothesizing, extracting general principles and be ready to test their reformulations against future practice. All these features can be considered to contribute towards becoming a reflective practitioner.

In many instances 'personal theory' becomes equated with 'professional thinking'. For, if theory and action are assumed to be related, then it can be assumed that thinking about professional activity should reveal the underlying personal theories and the ways in which professionals theorize about their practice. The particular interest in student/teacher 'planning' processes relates partly to the fact that this focus of personal theory and professional thinking is at the interface of belief and practice concerning what many would describe as the professional task — the act of classroom teaching. Interest in 'planning' may also relate to the fact that because it is central to the task of the teacher, it is often one of the most accessible aspects of the teacher's role and therefore easier to research. Because planning concerns thinking about action, it is possible to investigate the relation between the two. Where planning and action are followed by evaluation, it is possible to trace the links between intention, implementation, evaluation and refinement, and hence to monitor the reformulation (or otherwise) of personal theories.

However, in the case of these students the planning sections of their files were of limited interest in terms of throwing light upon their personal theories. This was mainly because the learning aims and objectives selected were justified in terms of being requirements of the National Curriculum. Little additional rationale was deemed necessary. It was the evaluations which proved to be of greater interest in throwing light on their theorizing processes and thus in the development of their own personal theories.

It would seem, therefore, that we ignore the student's personal theory at our peril, if we wish to understand students' pre-existing theories about teaching so that we can encourage them to explore both their own and others'. But, as the discussion below suggests, it also seems clear that to dwell on this exclusively would be to court disaster.

What Conditions Support the Development of the 'Reflective' Practitioner?

I have suggested so far that reflective practice requires the practitioner to elicit and identify their personal theories, to explore these by examining their rationale, by problematizing and looking for alternative analyses, then to compare these with peers and with public theories before attempting to re-formulate the theory and test it against further practice. The typical context for this is classroom fieldwork. However, if fieldwork experience is to contribute towards the dynamic development of theory it is necessary for students to adopt an open-minded attitude and to acquire very particular skills. It is the nature of experience to have implications which go far beyond what is first noted. But recognizing a potential 'moment of insight' requires a prepared mind. Dewey (1933) postulated that education can only happen through experience, but that only certain experiences are educative. Educative experience must be 'continuous' (i.e. relate to previous and subsequent experience) and be 'interactive' (i.e. the person acts upon the situation which in turn acts upon them). Dewey (1916) asserted that learning from experience is only possible if combined with rigorous use of a systematic experimental method. This requires a learner to observe, understand the significance of what they observe and to make judgments based on such understandings. 'Observations' need to be focused, not just on means-ends relationships, but on the relationships between means. The ends also need to be examined and their inter-relationships examined (Dewey, 1938).

The observers' skills in learning from observation depend on their capacity for critical discrimination and their ability to reason. Dewey argued that, in addition, the experimental method required that ideas and hypotheses needed to be generated from such observations and tested, and that these were to be judged by the consequences of being acted upon. He urged that it was important to 'keep track' of such testing (through recording, summarizing, reviewing), so that it was possible to 'reflect back' and extract meanings, and then to 'lead out' to increase understandings. Further: 'only if experience leads to an expanding of understanding is it educative ... [and if it] leads to an intelligent organization of these understandings' (1916, p. 112). 'Otherwise,' Dewey remarks, 'experience is chaotic and too dispersive.'

Others, such as Gitlin and Teitelbaum (1983), have similarly argued that by encouraging teachers to observe, step back, to utilize their understandings and to consider why certain practices occur they can examine their ethical and educational implications. It is then valuable to present the findings in a coherent form for discussion which can encourage students concretely and directly to integrate theory and practice. Such reflection allows the individual to free themselves of habitual ways of thinking, to transform perspectives and to establish belief on a firm basis of evidence and rationality (Mezirow, 1978, 1981; and Boud, 1985). However, the processes of critical self-reflection can be fraught with tensions and for this reason students need close support and frequent encouragement. Further, Anning (1988) points out how it is necessary for the student to feel they are in a secure emotional environment. They also need to be positively involved in decision-making in the classroom so they have some stake and ownership in the activities and to have the opportunity to explore open-ended tasks and responses, so they have a chance to act upon their reflections.

On What Criteria can Written Reflections be Appraised?

From the characteristics of reflection already suggested it could be possible to compile a checklist of criteria for analysing students' writings and discussions in order to monitor their development in reflective thinking.

Much can be made of the ambiguity surrounding 'reflection', but there is a growing literature which is clarifying the strategies and procedures which educationalists believe contribute successfully to developing the reflective practitioner. In culling the research for authors' perceived indicators for articulating such characteristics, it is possible to find a fair level of agreement in spirit, if not in terminology.

For example, with reference to lesson planning, Boud *et al.* (1985) suggests three phases. Based on these, one could list, in the preparation phase, the need:

- to identify aims (both educational aims and their relation to consequences for justice, equality and fulfilment (Van Manan, 1977) and the underlying ethical assumptions (Tom, 1988));

- to clarify requirements and review resources;
- to plan presentation strategies and participation roles;
- to explore their implications (and form hypotheses which can be tested in action (Dewey, 1938)).

In the second, engagement, phase (where Dewey emphasizes the need for 'keen observation'), critical and reflective writings would be expected to show:

- summary description of events (without judgment);
- sections of recorded dialogue, questioning, feedback, etc;
- some initial impressions and ideas for subsequent critical reflection.

The third and final processing phase is the most complex and demanding. Dewey states the need for 'reasoned analysis'. It is precisely this process of reconstruction, deconstruction and reformulation which needs de-mystifying. Contributory procedures might include:

- selection of a 'key' event;
- articulation of and working through associated emotions;
- problematization of event (by generating multiple causes and con-sequences through association and brainstorming so as to avoid the temptation of clinging to instant hunches (Mackinnon, 1987));
- crystallization of issues (categorization and interpretation of alterna-tive hypotheses (Boud, 1985));
- validation (testing for consistency, confirm interpretation with others, relate to previous learning, compare with others' experi-ences, consult available 'authorities' (Liston and Zeichner, 1990));
- appropriation (test understandings, extract and internalize signi-ficance, plan own further learning (Schön, 1987)).

By using such, or similar, procedures it could provide a structured framework for helping students into finding their own form of reflective thinking. Such strategies could help practitioners to 'overcome the limits of first-hand experience, through utilizing various conceptual tools and skills of enquiry which can help them to see beyond the immediate circumstances of their situation' (Zeichner, 1987).

To use such a framework for analysis of reflective writings could be useful for initial analysis, but might well miss rich insights into student think-ing which could be gained from more laborious content analysis. Holly and McLaughlin (1989) offer an alternative form of content analysis. They suggest that charting the themes and shifts in interpretations given by a student over time will reveal rich information about their changing personal theories. For example, the different aspects for which teachers praise chil-dren in the classroom reveals implicit 'theories' of their concept of a 'good pupil'. The differences in what the student focuses on in their own performance similarly reveals their changing concerns as well as possible changes in their conception of 'good teaching' and their response to the role of teacher. Holly and McLaughlin noted that frequent themes included teacher sense of isolation, issues pertaining to self-image and to role satisfaction.

Alternative initial short-cut procedures have also been suggested, using linguistic features as the basis for analysis. For example, in order to identify student reasoning it would be possible to mark up every use of conjunctions (such as 'because' 'so'), or the use of infinitive verbs and other indicators of purpose (such as 'in order to . . .'). Problematizing could be highlighted by counting the number of alternative causes/consequences evidenced by the above linguistic features in support of any single event (Mackinnon, 1987). A shift from mono-causal judgments to multi-causal interpretations could show a willingness to explore problems rather than to prejudge them. However, the validity of this approach depends on linguistic style: students often use note form, report forms with listed points. Much of the file would need to be 'rephrased' in terms of the deep-structure meanings expressed by the students before being amenable to analysis by surface linguistic features.

In addition, Wagner (1987) suggests that the relative balance between the use of the indicative and imperative mood gives clues as to the amount of description used (employing verbs in the indicative mood) compared to the decisions made — assuming this is the result of analysis and reflection? — (employing verbs in the imperative mood). Whilst linguistic features certainly can be useful clues, the validity of any linguistic analysis will be limited by the variety of writing styles used by students (e.g. whether they write in note form or full sentences), whether they elaborate their observations and responses or prefer to keep most of it 'in their heads'. Also, their writings only reflect their willingness and ability to write and not their ability to think, reason or theorize explicitly.

What are the Likely Student Concerns and How did the Students Respond?

For the purposes of this chapter, I will restrict the focus of personal theory to novice student teachers during their lesson planning and evaluation activities.

Despite so many variations in the planning processes, researchers have found patterns in student lesson planning in general. A number of studies have found that lesson planning is more likely to be based on teacher management concerns than on pupil learning criteria (Zahorik, 1975; Carter and Doyle, 1984; Mackinnon, 1987). This is hardly surprising given that students' main objectives are to 'survive' and to 'pass'. However, a closer investigation of the varying terms used in these studies reveals that important distinctions seem to be made between pupil interest and attitudes which are deemed to be related to 'management' (on the assumption that if the children aren't interested they are difficult to manage) and 'pupil learning criteria' which seem to include individual needs, task differentiation, alternative approaches to instruction, and of identifying task objectives and matching them to learner needs.

Mackinnon (1987) identifies initial concerns as being with relationships with children (with individuals as 'children'), which soon gave way to concern with management (where 'children' became 'pupils') and classroom materials, teacher explanations and methods are key features and, only later, do students feel able (and sufficiently familiar with the children) to focus on trying to meet individual learner needs. Hence, in general terms students appear to shift from being child orientated, to teacher orientated, to learner orientated.

Analysis

In analysing this sample of lesson plans and evaluations two particular features emerged: shifts in the reflective perspectives of the student (both in function and focus) and shifts in reasoning processes (both quantitively and qualitatively).

Shifts in Reflective Perspective

i) Function

Students initially tended to adopt a retrospective stance and to review the session just completed in terms of whether the 'lesson went well'. This first stage, of very general and rather superficial evaluation, was usually highly descriptive and often couched in terms of child-orientated judgments with little or no evidence or reasoning.

> e.g. 'It was hard work. The children were noisy.'
> 'We were pleased with the session and the children followed our plans.'

These statements were not elaborated and appeared to be presented as self-evident.

This unsubstantiated 'evaluation' soon gave way to the second stage of 'explanation', where implicit reasons emerged into explicit reasons and where immediate individualized cause or consequence was elaborated by reference to situational context and circumstances.

> e.g. 'There was chaos because all the children tried to glue simultaneously and there were not enough resources to share.'

'They weren't used to group work so they found it hard to collaborate.'

'The gale made them really excited so I switched plans and did some weather poems, individually, instead.'

There was also increasing evidence of students learning from their experience and making reasoned resolutions which were pro-active, or 'prospective', leading to reformulated purposes to underpin future planning.

e.g. 'Our objectives for next week had to change to retain control.'

A third stage revealed 'exploration' and a willingness to examine alternative possible causes/consequences, to problematize and hypothesize and to raise issues relating to generalizable principles of practice.

e.g. 'Because I kept a tight structure, perhaps the children began to rely on me too much, perhaps they lacked confidence, perhaps I didn't explain clearly enough and hindered their learning, perhaps the task was too open.'

'How do I keep children enthusiastic but without letting them get disruptive? Does there always have to be a battle between motivation and control?'

ii) Focus

There was also a change in the focus of the comments. At first remarks were 'self-orientated' and related to their own particular situation and incidents reported were described as it affected them personally.

e.g. 'The noise meant that all sensible communication was impossible. I was overwhelmed. IT MUST NEVER HAPPEN AGAIN.'

'I must remember to separate K and W. They are not good for each other . . . or for me.'

Next, students were able to 'stand back', compare different strategies and learn from each other or from the classroom teacher and become more 'peer orientated'.

e.g. 'I noticed [teacher] M stopped the discussion (which was getting rowdy) and reminded the children of the rules they devised earlier. I wish I'd done that last week . . . it made them stop and think AND take responsibility for their own behaviour, collectively . . .'

Later, students began to link personal experience with the public domain of texts. Such 'public orientated' consultation was not frequent and it was mostly used to confirm their own ideas rather than to challenge them.

Table 4.1   showing changing patterns of response in the development of student personal theory during first-year evaluations of serial practice, given as percentages of number of 'theorizing' items in their reflective file.

	Unsubstantiated judgments	Implicit reasons	Explicit reasons	Problematizing	Consulting references
'Infant'					
Week 1	18%	34%	44%	2%	1%
Week 4	10%	23%	49%	9%	7%
'Junior'					
Week 1	17%	35%	35%	10%	2%
Week 4	11%	34%	40%	5%	10%

e.g.   'It is important to pre-empt trouble through 'withitness', as Kounin defines it.'

For these first year students, the personal-public linkages were tentative but a start had been made which might allow them to explore alternative perspectives which might help to overcome the 'limitations of experience'.

Shifts in Reasoning Processes

i)   Quantitative

There was a marked change overall in both the number and distribution of reasoning as evidenced in the students' files over the four weeks of school visits. Table 4.1 demonstrates students' increasing willingness and ability to search for reasons for their actions and to look for reasons in the children's behaviour. It also shows that the students became increasingly open-minded regarding their search for alternative explanations concerning children's responses to the classroom activities. Students also became more adept at generating a range of hypotheses about their own future strategies and showed greater confidence in exploring alternative possibilities. Some of them found time to consult public theory and to compare this with their own personal theories, though the use of references was not often, at this stage, particularly critical.

However, what was of greater interest was the differences in the nature of the reasons which were given. In particular there was a considerable difference between those students working with junior-aged children (8–9 years) compared with those working with infants (6–7 years). The junior students clearly found 'control' a major concern. It was also a concern in the infant classrooms. But whereas the junior students defined it as a threat to their position and authority and responded in terms of the need for discipline, the infant students defined it as a problem of matching and responded in terms of the need for task differentiation. Thus the junior students were more 'teacher-orientated' while the infant students were more 'learner-orientated'. Maybe the age — and size — of the children meant that the younger ones were perceived as less threatening. Maybe the younger ones were more distractable or more biddable.

ii) Qualitative

The initial impressions on reading the student evaluations were, first of all, that they began by being written in a 'story' style: the texts were in narrative form and told the story of the lesson as it happened. This appeared to be a necessary stage for students to experience before they could begin to see patterns, trends, recurrent issues which could then form the basis of a more analytic approach. The initial evaluations were more like annotated commentaries, which were frequently insightful and began to explore causes and consequences of events as well as of future planning. These commentaries did not make use of any theoretical frameworks or constructs for facilitating and extending analysis which might also lead them from personal to public theory.

Another marked feature of the evaluations was that they each identified negative aspects of the learning sessions: in only two occasions were positive or successful aspects of the student's teaching strategies mentioned. Clearly it was what 'went wrong' which concerned them most and they found it easy to get 'mistakes' out of proportion.

Further, as the students became more familiar with the evaluation process, the over-emphasis on negative evaluation shifted to a more equal balance between 'evaluation', 'resolution' regarding modified strategies about how to teach and also changes in 'rationale' concerning what to teach for future sessions. The students appeared to become better able to put evaluation to positive use and showed they could learn from their experience. Thus the 'session review' lead them through the 'reflective cycle' and into 'reformulated planning'. The strategies by which they demonstrated these changes illustrated many of the ones identified by Boud (1985). Thus the evaluations showed the students' 'engagement' stage (through the description, recording of evidence and personal responses), followed by the students' 'processing' stage (reasoned analysis and problematization). Where the students outlined resolutions they demonstrated further processing (crystallization, validation and appropriation). Whilst in their rationale sections they demonstrated their planning and 'preparation' stage.

Evaluation: The evaluation statements fell into a number of different categories which shifted in prominence through the following sets of criteria. At first students were 'child-orientated' and were tempted to 'blame' the pupils if things went 'wrong' often in terms of their personalities.

e.g. 'The survey didn't work well because the children were too selfish to be able to work together.'
'There was too much disruption because the children kept wandering around and nosing into everybody else's tasks.'

Often the next stage was to become teacher-orientated and to 'blame' themselves, especially in relation to the criteria of control.

> e.g. 'It got chaotic with four "teachers", as no one knew which was really "in charge".'

Poor communication skills were also frequently cited, in terms of style of interaction, quality of explanations or clarity of expectations.

> e.g. 'They didn't respond well to open questions so I switched to closed.'
> 'They all drew pictures instead of a design because I didn't really explain the difference properly.'
> 'It was too noisy because we didn't establish the kind of behaviour which we wanted.'

Attention to management skills became a later focus, in particular issues of pacing, or distribution and use of teacher time.

> e.g. 'The introduction took too long so we didn't have time to finish the follow up work.'
> 'I found it hard with two groups as they both wanted me all the time.'

The use of materials was also mentioned as causing problems.

> e.g. 'They wouldn't share the cards, so I had to deal them out equally to each child.'

The last and least frequent focus to be mentioned in trying to identify 'why the session went wrong' was in terms of being learner-orientated. This minority group of students paid more attention to the children as learners. They tried to consider opportunities for differentiation, for motivation, for task matching and for identifying individual needs relating to competencies and cognitive skills, rather than just personality.

> e.g. 'Some couldn't write independently, so I wrote and then they copied.'
> 'They enjoyed the practical activities as they seemed novel and fun.'
> 'The children estimated "danger" in terms of the quantity of cars as this was something they could see (concrete) rather than as speed or weight (more abstract).'
> 'I had to make it more structured as the openness seem to confuse. Open questions were profitable as it gave children a greater opportunity of control over the task, but many were not used to it.'

Resolutions: These moved from an understandable obsession with survival, to greater attention to procedural strategies and then to critical pedagogy.

i) Survival: particular events, context specific, short-term outcomes.

>e.g. control: 'I'll withdraw my group next week to reduce the noise levels.'
>communication: 'I need to explain more about "design" to avoid confusion.'
>management: 'I need more filler activities (!) to occupy the children.'
>materials: 'I'll reduce the number of children needing the same resources, to avoid wasted-time.'

ii) Procedural: identifying generalizable teaching strategies, generating underlying principles. This was often as a result of close observation and use of tape recordings of student-pupil talk, or diary notes by peer students whilst the target student led the whole class for an introduction/discussion, or a tally sheet used by the students whilst monitoring their group of pupils.

>e.g. control: 'Need more careful use of questioning to structure positive and disciplined discussions and stop calling out.'
>communication: 'Need to simplify instructions and talk more slowly.'
>management: 'Smaller groups would allow a greater amount of participation.'
>materials: 'Need to have a visual reminder of task instructions and not just rely on my verbal explanations.'

iii) Critical: relating to children's needs and long-term consequences. These seemed to reflect selected issues picked up from directed readings.

>e.g. learner needs: 'There seem to be too many work sheets which have more to do with control than learning.'
>learner outcomes: 'Do these activities reflect the children's needs? Do they see the point, or does it turn them off?'
>'How does the atmosphere of the classroom affect the child's self-esteem?'
>'What are they learning about "being a pupil"? What kind of future are they being prepared for?'

Rationale: The students were given selected attainment targets (ATs) by the schools which they were expected to incorporate in their plans so as to fit in with that term's topic. The students had also been encouraged, by the Polytechnic, to try broadly to relate their sessions around the theme of 'health and safety'. This was so that a common ground would exist for content discussion and because past experience had proved that this theme was popular in the schools. It appears that with so many 'givens' acting as constraints, it discouraged students from delving too deeply in the whys and wherefores of what they planned.

The students made a number of assumptions regarding the basic premises for selecting their teaching content and methods. It appeared that 'to encourage independence' was a key priority in almost all groups. This was broken down into subsidiary aims such as:

- 'to learn how to find out for themselves' (through discussion and experiences of reference books);
- 'to develop self-esteem and confidence' (through eliciting and valuing children's opinions);
- 'to engage them/make it fun' (through active participation which was also expected to motivate and make the experiences more memorable and also to contribute to manageability).

Students predominantly chose the knowledge which they wished the children to acquire rather than consider skills or ATs, though these were never far from their minds. 'Knowledge' ranged from nutrition to food chains, or care of pets to care of the environment. But in every instance, the sequencing appeared to move from what was 'familiar', 'near at hand' and concrete to what was less familiar, from secondary resources and more 'abstract'. There appears to be an implicit Piagetian and Brunerian influence at work here though neither were attributed in the planning sessions or the final reflections upon their planning processes. The sequencing was regarded as 'natural' and 'obvious': such knowledge was regarded as being intrinsically 'worthwhile' and therefore necessary to inculcate.

Skills which were emphasized included those of a 'social' nature, such as collaboration and group discussion, as well as of a 'cognitive' nature, such as investigation, interpretation and imagination. It was stated that these skills were 'fundamental' to learning and therefore 'necessary'.

The specific activities chosen as vehicles for this learning were selected on the basis of being 'relevant' and 'interesting'. 'Relevant' was seen as synonymous with 'familiar' and 'from the child's experience'. For example, one group started their investigations concerning nutrition with examining the children's lunch boxes, whilst the group wishing to investigate their understanding of caring for pets began with a discussion of the children's pets — only to discover that this was not a universal component of every household, which reduced one or two of the infants to tears.

In general the planning sections revealed far less detail about student thinking and their personal theories. It was the evaluations which proved to be richer. However, the subsequent plans were interesting in that they revealed the extent to which some students were able to alter their original plans in the light of what they had learnt from their previous week's experience through the process of 'review, reason, research, reflect and reformulate'.

Conclusions

Because 'personal theory' is so embedded in the way each of us thinks, students found it very hard to articulate and, if articulated implicitly, they found it very hard to spot the assumptions and to challenge them. Tutors needed to demand reasons by constantly probing with 'why', 'how do you know', 'so what', 'and next . . .'. A second area of difficulty for the students was in challenging their beliefs and practice. Tutors needed to encourage close observation by the individual student or in peer-pairs or through novice-expert discussion to enable them to explore the disparity between belief and practice and between alternative practices. Thirdly, students experienced great difficulty in making a personal-public link. Students explained that 'we don't know the words'. As first years, they were not familiar with the professional educational terminology. This meant that they had difficulty in articulating their experiences in anything other than colloquial terms, conceptualizing their comments and, literally, in 'looking things up in the index' of a text so that they could 'tune into the public theory'. This appears to be something that needs to be addressed early on in a course to provide students with a language with which they can share their personal experience and learn from others' public experiences. Without this prerequisite reflection can hardly begin.

References

ANNING, A. (1988) 'Teachers' theories about children's learning' in CALDERHEAD, J. (ed.) *Teachers' Professional Learning*, Lewes: Falmer Press.

ARKOFF, R. (1979) 'The future of operational research is past', *Journal of Operational Research*, **30**, pp. 93–104.

BERLINER, D.C. (1987) 'Ways of thinking about students and classrooms', in CALDERHEAD, J. (ed.) *Exploring Teachers' Thinking*, London: Cassell.

BOUD, D., KEOGH, R. and WALKER, D. (eds) (1985) 'Promoting reflection in learning: a model', in BOUD, D. (ed.) *Reflection: Turning Experience into Learning*, London: Kogan Page.

CALDERHEAD, J. (ed.) (1987) *Exploring Teacher's Thinking*, London: Cassell.

— (ed.) (1988) *Teachers' Professional Learning*, Lewes: Falmer Press.

CARR, W. and KEMMIS, S. (1986) *Becoming Critical: Education, Knowledge and Action Research*, Lewes: Falmer Press.

CARTER, K. and DOYLE, W. (1984) 'Variations in academic tasks in high and average ability classes' in LOMES, L. (ed.) *Classroom Research*, Victoria, Australia: Deakin University Press.

COPELAND, W. (1980) 'Student teachers and cooperating teachers', *Theory into Practice*, **18**, pp. 194–199.

DEWEY, J. (1916) *Democracy and Education*, New York: Macmillan.

— (1933) *How We Think*, Chicago: Henry Regnery.

— (1938) *Experience and Education*, Kappa Delta Pi.

ELY, M. *et al.* (1991) *Doing Qualitative Research*, Lewes: Falmer Press.

GITLIN, A. and TEITELBAUM, K. (1983) 'Linking theory to practice', *Journal of Education for Teaching*, **9**, 3, pp. 225–234.

GOODMAN, J. (1984) 'Reflection and teacher education', *Interchange*, **15**, 3, pp. 9–26.

HOLLY, M.L. and McLAUGHLIN, C.S. (1989) (eds) *Perspectives on Teacher Professional Development*, Lewes: Falmer Press.

JOHNSON, K. (1988) 'Changing teacher's conceptions of teaching and learning', in CALDERHEAD, J. (ed.) *Teachers' Professional Learning*, Lewes: Falmer Press.

LISTON, D. and ZEICHNER, K. (1990) 'Reflective teaching and action research in preservice teacher education', *Journal of Education for Teaching*, **16**, 3, pp. 235–254.

MACKINNON, A. (1987) 'Detecting reflection-in-action among pre-service teachers', *Teacher and Teacher Education*, **3**, 2, pp. 135–145.

MEZIROW, J. (1978) 'Perspective Transformations', *Adult Education*, **28**, 2, pp. 100–110.

— (1981) 'A critical theory of adult learning and education', *Adult Education*, **32**, 1, pp. 3–24.

SCHÖN, D. (1983) *The Reflective Practitioner*, New York: Basic Books.

— (1987) *Educating the Reflective Practitioner*, San Francisco: Jossey-Bass.

TOM, A.R. (1988) 'Replacing pedagogical knowledge with pedagogical questions', in SMYTH, J. (ed.) *Educating Teachers*, Lewes: Falmer Press.

WAGNER, A. (1987) 'Knots in teacher thinking', in CALDERHEAD, J. (ed.) *Exploring Teachers' Thinking*, London: Cassell.

WALKER, D. (1985) 'Writing and Reflection', in BOUD, D. (ed.) *Reflection: Turning Experience into Learning*, London: Kogan Page.

ZAHORIK, D. (1975) 'Teachers' planning models', *Educational Leadership*, **33**, pp. 134–139.

ZEICHNER, K.M. *et al.* (1987) 'Individual, institutional and cultural influences in teacher education', in CALDERHEAD, J. (ed.) *Exploring Teachers' Thinking*, London: Cassell.

ZEICHNER, K.M. and GRANT, C.K. (1981) 'Biography and social structures in the socialization of student-teachers', *Journal of Education for Teaching*, **7**, pp. 298–314.

ZEICHNER, K.M. and LISTON, D. (1990) 'Reflective teaching and action research in preservice teacher education', *Journal of Education for Teachers*, **16**, 3, pp. 235–254.

5 Life-History Accounts as Mirrors: A Practical Avenue for the Conceptualization of Reflection in Teacher Education

J. Gary Knowles

Life-history research is rich and arresting. Indeed, life histories as told to researchers have provided backbones to some of the more illuminating and persuasive anthropological and sociological research of this century (see e.g. Bertaux, 1981; Denzin, 1989; Watson and Watson-Franke, 1985; Wiley, 1986). Life-history accounts have illuminated aspects of particular cultures — even whole cultures — in significant ways (see e.g. Dyk, 1938; Freeman, 1979; Radin, 1926; Shostak, 1981; Simmons, 1942; Shaw, 1966), including the cultures of education, schools, and teachers (see e.g. Becker, 1952; Beynon, 1985; Goodson, 1981, 1983). They are, therefore, not completely foreign to the examination of pertinent professional and personal issues in education and, as such, have been used with particular success in examining aspects of teaching practices, curriculum, and school histories (see e.g. Ball and Goodson, 1985; Beynon, 1985; Goodson, 1991; Knowles and Holt-Reynolds, 1991; Smith, Dwyer, Prunty and Kleine, 1988; Woods, 1984).

Life histories are also illuminating windows on the processes of reflection that prospective teachers have utilized throughout their long experience of being students. As personal constructs, life histories access the impact of these experiences on the thinking of teachers in preparation. In this chapter I explore the usefulness of personal histories as a kind of mirror through which both preservice teachers and teacher educators can view the origins of preservice teachers' personal perspectives about teaching, classrooms, schools and education. It draws on a small body of work which explores preservice teachers' perspectives within the context of their life histories. Further, considering my own professional experiences associated with creating, sharing and analyzing personal histories in preservice teacher education, I suggest that personal history accounts, coupled with extended conversations about the substance of those accounts, provides one avenue for conceptualizing and implementing reflective inquiry in preservice teacher education. In the process I define life histories and life-history accounts in teacher education, explore the tasks associated with constructing and examining life-history accounts, and relate the elements of life-history accounts to the process of reflective inquiry. All this underscores my advocacy for developing refined reflexive practice in prospective teachers which, in a sense, implies a refining of the reflexive practices that such individuals have engaged in the assessment of their own experiences as students.

Defining Life History: Applications and Functions in Research

My research preparation is steeped in the orientations and methods of anthropology and sociology, and it is from these perspectives that I first explored the potential of life histories as a means of finding answers to and meanings from the particular research questions that I asked in my work. For example, I especially found informant-constructed life-history accounts invaluable for exploring home education — where parents take on the responsibility of educating their children at home (see e.g. Knowles, 1989b, 1991a). I also found life-history accounts helpful for exploring the relationships between life experiences associated with the long period of 'apprenticeship of observation' (Lortie, 1975) — experiences of learning and observing classrooms and teachers in schools — and the practices of beginning teachers (see e.g. Knowles, 1992, 1989a; Knowles and Hoefler, 1989; Knowles and Holt-Reynolds, 1991).

To extend the use of the life-history method beyond the purposes of research to formal teacher preparation was a natural progression in my thinking, given my preservice teacher education responsibilities (see Knowles, 1991b), and my research interest in the early period of teacher development and socialization. Others, such as Goodson and Cole (1991), and Sikes and Aspinwall (1990), have also found life histories particularly productive in this area of study. My knowledge and use of the method as a research tool greatly influenced my pedagogy (Knowles and Holt-Reynolds, 1991) and, as a result, I developed an appropriate definition of life histories and, eventually, a schemata for the use of the life-history method in preservice teacher education classes that I taught.

A Definition

Life history accounts are one distinctive form of personal documents, like autobiographies, diaries and journals, and artistic expressions such as novels and poetry, and painting and sculpture:

> Personal documents as a generic category include any expressive production of the individual that can be used to throw light on his

view of himself, his life situation, or the state of the world as he understands it, at some particular point in time or over the passage of time (Watson and Watson-Franke, 1985, p. 2).

As a category of personal documents, life histories are distinguished by the motivations associated with the recording of the life: 'As we see it the "life history" is any retrospective account by the individual of his life in whole or in part, in written or oral form, that has been elicited or prompted by another person' (Watson and Watson-Franke, 1985, p. 2). In other words, life-history accounts, whether in written or spoken form, are constructed at the request of someone other than the person the life history describes. This definition undergirds the use of life-history accounts as I describe them in the remainder of this chapter. Also, I use the terms 'life history' and 'personal history' interchangeably.

Applications

There are, as is to be expected within the disparate applications of anthropology and sociology, various interpretive modes applied to and associated with life-history research (see e.g. Denzin, 1989; Watson and Watson-Franke, 1985). But, for the purposes of using life-history accounts in teacher preparation programs, the meanings attributed to prior experiences are those assigned by the 'story tellers' or writers themselves — preservice teachers. In that vein, the interpretations are akin to phenomenological explorations of the subjective experience (Watson and Watson-Franke, 1985; see also Van Manen, 1989). Emerging from those self-interpretations, in tandem with engaging dialogues about teaching with more experienced individuals, is the extension and development of productive schema for working with students within school classrooms. In this way, preservice teachers extend the boundaries of their personal knowledge in furthering their own professional development.

Functions

With respect to the value of the life-history research method for enlightening understandings of education, Beynon (1985), drawing on the work of Faraday and Plummer (1979), Bogdan and Taylor (1970), Dollard (1949), and Becker (1966), succinctly notes three functions, each of which are beneficial in the present context — that of using life-history accounts in preservice teacher education. The first is a subjective function:

> The life history method is uniquely placed to grapple with the individual's subjective reality, assumptions and beliefs. It emphasizes

the interpretations people place on their everyday experiences as an explanation of behavior (Beynon, 1985, p. 164).

The second function is a contextual one. The life history locates an individual's life within a greater sphere: '[It] grounds the individual life in both the context of the lived experience as well as within the broader social and economic system in which s/he lives' (p. 164). Third, life histories have an evaluative function: 'The life history method reasserts the complexities of lived experience and alerts researchers to issues of which there is, as yet, a poor conceptualization.' (p. 165). In part, I interpret the evaluative function as implying the usefulness of life histories for exploring issues for which there are limited knowledge bases. While this function serves my research admirably, it also serves prospective teachers — and teacher educators — by drawing attention to the origins and conceptualizations of prospective teachers' thinking about working in classrooms.

The Nature, Substance and Usefulness of Life-History Accounts in Teacher Education

In developing a conceptualization of reflection in teacher education based on the examination of the nature and substance of life-history accounts that preservice teachers write, there are several elements which build upon the functions of the life-history method. I wish to lay these out in some detail; they form the infrastructure of my proposition. First, whether or not we (as teacher educators) recognize and acknowledge it, all prospective teachers possess rich, illuminating, intensely interesting personal histories; lives are full of interesting experiences, even though some individuals may claim the contrary for their lives and the lives of others. Second, although the process of writing ongoing personal histories is of itself useful, it is an activity which can sometimes be very difficult, perplexing and enervating. This is particularly so when writers confront elements of their prior experiences which are contradictory to elements of their present lives, career directions, or the philosophical orientations of teacher education programs and school placements within which they are immersed. Third, personal histories — not including chronologies of events — are, of the most part, private mental constructs unless they can be shared with other, trusted people in some form and, in this regard, a written format is useful. Thus, in the context of preservice teacher education, the process and product of writing, sharing, and elaborating the elements of one's personal history reflect or mirror the beliefs, actions, practices, skills and thinking which preservice teachers bring with them to formal preparation programs. For this reason, especially, the process has value for professional development.

Rich and Intensely Interesting

People lead interesting lives. And, they usually enjoy telling stories about critical, memorable instances of their lives around dinner tables, at social events, in times of nostalgia, on occasions which celebrate life — and death — and, indeed, at any time when other people will listen or are a captive audience. Hospital and physicians' waiting rooms, carriages in railway trains, saloons in hotels and ocean liners, bars in local pubs, places where strangers are brought together, places where people are united in some commonly-experienced event or circumstance — by chance or intent — are all places where elements of personal histories are told and retold. In the process of telling their life stories, individuals raise their consciousness about the substance and meanings of life circumstances and events (see e.g. Meyerhoff, 1982).

Usually, listeners are passive — as in the story teller's captive audience in the carriage booth on a moving train or the unsuspecting traveller in the shared seat on a long intercontinental bus journey. Often, on occasions of passive listening, stories are found wanting of substance, sequence, linkages, logic, convergence or consequence — and, in most cases, listeners do not question the integrity of stories. Less often, listeners actively seek to resolve anomalies and obtain clarification of points made by the story teller. On such occasions, questions of story tellers often help make life stories more coherent, more internally consistent. But always, whether stories hang together or not, they are usually more intensely interesting as a result of calls for clarification.

Stories that are internally consistent or focused are particularly arresting, especially if they tell elements of life histories that witness challenges and confrontations, changes and consequences, convergence and contradiction in contexts and conditions which represent the commonplace. Schools are commonplaces, environments that have and represent shared meanings for most people — unless, of course, you happen to have been home-educated by your parents. As such, stories about schools and classrooms, teachers and fellow pupils, form the basis of many elements of most preservice teachers' thinking about the professional practice of teaching — and of experienced teachers' practice (see e.g. Witherell and Noddings, 1991).

For young first-career preservice teachers, school experiences are often relatively vivid in their memories — after all, they are very recent. While older, second-career teachers in preparation may have less clear recollections of their own elementary and secondary school experiences, they, like their younger counterparts, may also draw from their experiences of schools, classrooms, and teachers as parents. And, as Pillemer, Goldsmith, Panter and White (1988), Pillemer (1984), and White (1982) point out, when long-past experiences were difficult or troublesome, individuals' recollections may not always be reliable. Nevertheless, individuals draw meaning from those recollections whether or not they are accurate in detail or spirit.

Confrontations with Contradictions

Writing life history accounts is often a difficult and exhausting task as writers recount, interconnect and make meaning of their past experiences. For some individuals, life histories often contain stories within stories, accounts that people sometimes prefer to forget or to place in the unreachable recesses of their minds. As such, some events are not always readily visible or accessible in normal conversation and may require a trigger for release. These less memorable topics are, however, often important sources for understanding the schemas through which the world is viewed.

For example, as I tried on various roles as a young beginning teacher there were certain cloaks of practice that did not match the rest of my attire — they did not jibe with the kinds of experiences I knew to be most valuable to *me* as a student — and I tended to dismiss them as being not appropriate for the wardrobe of my teaching repertoire. Why? On deeper examination, in some cases, the particular practices in question were connected to approaches or experiences with which or through which I had suffered (such as at the hands of an unethical teacher) or which were associated with punishment or near failure. In other cases, the practices did not resonate with me because of idiosyncratic perspectives or particular persons or circumstances that I associated with the specific practice. I simply did not like the practice or the student-required skills and activities that were associated with it. These kinds of dichotomies and dilemmas in one's think-ing in the early stages of professional development are often difficult to identify, address and write about in life-history accounts. On one hand a professor or classroom professional may have sworn by the usefulness of an approach while on the other hand I instantly rejected its usefulness, and explorations of my reasoning provided important insights into myself and the nature of my experiences.

Over the course of half-a-dozen years in which I have asked preservice teachers to explore their personal histories in written form, there have been a few individuals who have vehemently objected to the task. These objections were not necessarily because they saw the task as intrusive or time-consuming. Neither were the objections simply because the individuals experienced blocks in their attempts to write — although they probably did. Typically, and in private, these prospective teachers confided that their objections to writing were either grounded in events to which they attribute meanings contradictory to the direction of their current thinking or they were meanings that engendered painful and difficult experiences associated with learning and schools. In the first case they typically attributed meanings to events or circumstances which revealed massive internal inconsistencies in their thinking about teaching, classrooms, schools, and education, and about their very presence in programs of preservice teacher education within schools of education.

The preservice teachers' objections, then, were embedded in elements of their life histories that *they* recognized needed to be openly confronted and dealt with head on; but, they were very reluctant to do so. The polemical experience of writing life-history accounts seemed to offer nothing but pain. Translating intent into action is difficult indeed for some individuals under these kinds of circumstances.

Several individuals come to mind as providing illustrations of the confrontational aspects of writing life histories. One such person was Kathryn (a pseudonym) who, taking one of my courses, was particularly resistant to writing her life-history account. Kathryn was a young, idealistic, prospective teacher and a self-declared social reconstructivist long before she entered formal teacher education. She was an able writer, an English major with a particular flair for using innovative and student-centered approaches in the classroom, and a very proficient preservice teacher. She was well able to argue pedagogical theories and integrate them into her practice. She was purposeful and diligent about her preparation to become a new teacher; yet, she found it extremely difficult to write her life-history account and kept delaying its completion and presentation to me.

What made the writing of Kathryn's personal history particularly difficult was, she said: 'the finality of putting my thoughts down on paper.' She was referring to her delay in resolving the dilemmas posed by her contradictory experiences of schools, of teachers, and of learning. In effect she had not, until that particular point in time, tried to resolve some long-standing contradictory issues present in her thinking about public schools and their worth, and she intuitively knew that in the act of writing she would reveal those contradictions and inconsistencies in her own thinking about teaching. On the one hand, she had been exposed to 'fairly ordinary, dull teaching' by individuals who 'were themselves dull, boring and totally uncreative.' These individuals represented her summary impression of most teachers. In contrast, on the other hand, she learned a great deal about creativity, societal concerns and teachers' work from a singularly 'outstanding teacher', a woman who 'went to great pains to inspire a working-class, ordinary kid, to greater heights.' And this person was a kind of role model, somewhat a representation of her image of self as teacher (see Knowles, 1992).

To make things more confusing, Kathryn's working-class background and neighborhood, and elementary school experiences, did not prepare her for attending junior and high schools with students from middle- and upper-middle-class families. The resulting experience was one of isolation, loneliness, frustration, pain and ostracization. She resorted to 'fostering solid relationships with a few adults' who not only 'spoke [her] language and understood [her]' but also provided stimulating discussions and exhibited enthusiastic learning about many contrasting aspects of the local community. These, indeed, were confusing experiences and, as a result, the prospect of writing about herself within a framework connected to the heart of her thinking about education loomed ominously overhead.

Kathryn had delayed dealing with the contrasting experiences in other than 'the relatively superficial ways that [she] had made meaning from [them] as a younger adult.' As a result, she was totally ambivalent about the value of public schools, their place in contemporary communities, and their value for providing equal opportunities and creative experiences. These unresolved philosophical and intellectual issues were at the heart of her resistance to writing her life history.

Kathryn's case illustrates some of the difficulties and kinds of internal contradictions that constrain writers. Yet, for those who manage to overcome these kinds of internal constraints (as Kathryn eventually did when she was freed of the boundaries and expectations established by the activity as an impending course requirement), writing life histories and subsequently sharing them can be particularly illuminating and beneficial for those involved. In Kathryn's parting words, after she had completed the onerous task:

> Writing my autobiography [meaning life history] was particularly difficult. It was hell! After putting it off for so long [— some six months —] it felt particularly good to lay out in the open the issues that had bothered me for so long. Not only that, but I was able to re-examine the constructs of my positions and some of them — really quite a few — were ill-founded or based on incomplete information and limited experiences.

Expressions of Private Mental Constructs

As Kathryn illustrated in her own words, she not only thought of her life-history account as 'a window on my thinking about being a teacher' but as a 'revelation of who I am, ... of the [teaching] methods that I hold close to my heart, and of the ones that I detest in teachers' [practice].' Likewise, Watson and Watson-Franke (1985) and others such as Allport (1942), Becker (1966), Denzin (1989), and Langness and Frank (1981), argue that a central value and usefulness of life histories, in the context of research activities, is that they lay bare the thinking of the narrator or writer.

Life-history accounts offer a vehicle for gaining insights into private mental constructs. The process yields useful information for both writers and readers. Because of their form, life-history accounts offer a degree of convenience for readers — as observers or instructors in the context of preservice teacher education — to understand those with whom they work. Simultaneously, the act of writing personal accounts induces preservice teachers to be careful and cognizant in the act of revealing their thinking — since written accounts demand high levels of internal consistency and clarification because of the typical expectations associated with university papers and assignments. But, in the act of writing life-history accounts, perspectives and circumstances are frozen in time. This presents limitations to the scope of mental constructs revealed since writers have control over the windows through which they allow others to view. As such, while the thinking is laid bare, it may only represent partial perspectives. There is a need, therefore, to go beyond the initial explication, to further examine and extend the articulated constructs. Dialogue journals (to be discussed later) provide one vehicle for construction clarification.

What are some of the mental constructs that are viewed? Personal histories, whether in written or spoken form, reveal the *internal dialogues* about teaching and schools that preservice teachers use. These dialogues are the result of mostly long-held beliefs about teaching and working in classrooms, a product of a long apprenticeship of observation (Lortie, 1975). When thinking about teaching practices and classroom teaching, preservice teachers tend to access their own experiences, and on the basis of their assessment of worth accept or reject them. They do this by conducting mental discussions about such practices by trying them out on various real and imaginary students and themselves as students. Questions such as 'How would I react to this practice?' or 'What would my friend have done in this circumstance?' precipitate a mental discussion or dialogue with that real or imagined person about the value of the teaching method. Within these dialogues are *practical arguments* about theory and practice relevant to working with students in classrooms and schools. These represent the substance of the internal dialogues that are the very basis for accepting or rejecting a particular practice as being suitable for them. For example, rejection of a particular strategy for maintaining classroom order may simply be 'One of my teachers used to use this method and I hated it because . . . therefore I refuse to use it.' Or, . . . 'This is a useful way of teaching . . . because it allows kids to take charge and that's what I appreciated as a learner.' A more detailed account of internal dialogues and practical arguments as I use the concept is found in Knowles and Holt-Reynolds, 1991 (see also Holt-Reynolds, 1990; Knowles, 1990).

Unless teacher educators take special efforts to converse extensively with preservice teachers, a very difficult task when confronted with teaching and facilitating the development of large numbers of them, the private mental constructs of preservice teachers are likely to remain largely that — private, hidden, or camouflaged. As a result, the potential of such examination for informing practice is left unrealized.

Further, the life-history accounts illustrate a kind of reflection in operation. The mental constructs — the internal dialogues and practical arguments — are evidence of considerable analyses of teachers, teaching, classrooms and schools since they record the impacts of long associations with schools. Moreover, the subsequent explorations of those experiences by the writers themselves represent elements of a more refined, systematic reflective inquiry and these activities also present many opportunities for professional development.

Developing the Substance of Conversations:
The Task of Constructing Life-History Accounts

The implicit task of asking preservice teachers to construct life-history accounts is to develop a basis for a continued conversation — making the implicit explicit — about the nature and substance of their thinking (Knowles and Holt-Reynolds, 1991). To encourage prospective teachers in the writing of their personal history accounts I use a combination of approaches. For example, I attempt to: 1) develop open, safe, and respectful learning environments within small peer groups; 2) accept and openly acknowledge personal experiences as valuable for informing theories and practices of teaching; 3) acknowledge and model the value of discussing shared experiences of classrooms and schools; 4) share accounts of my life history — or elements of it — in written and oral forms (see Knowles and Holt-Reynolds, 1991); 5) extensively discuss the nature, substance, and value of constructing life-history accounts; 6) acknowledge the difficulty of writing and provide alternative structures, topics or questions for hesitant writers; and, 7) expect the assignment to be completed in almost *any* way that promotes the growth of individuals' professional knowledge and skills, and *their* satisfaction with the completed account and process.

In the context of courses I teach, the life-history assignments are usually fashioned by providing preservice teachers with a written statement about the value and usefulness of exploring elements of their life histories, followed by a list of topics and questions that are designed to promote responses and thinking about the substance of prior experiences. The life histories are not intended to be chronological accounts of events — although they may include such — but, rather, are insightful examinations of their efforts to become teachers within the contexts of their educational lives. Potentially useful topics include: decisions to become a teacher; teachers' work; visions of teachers and teaching; outstanding teachers and their influence; metaphors for teaching and working with students in classrooms; learning styles and opportunities; conflicts about the nature of schools and their organization; doubts about self-as-teacher; the influence of class, race, society, location on educational experiences; and, relations with teachers, students and persons of handicap. In summary, as stated in one of the course outlines requiring written life-history accounts:

A purposeful and forthright life history/personal history will address personal and formative experiences relating to learning, education and schools, besides acknowledging biases and the impact of negative role models, negative attitudes and stereotypical viewpoints. Philosophical positions about education in general, discipline, classroom management, curriculum orientations, extracurricular activities and other aspects of learning and teaching, probably ought to be addressed (Knowles, 1989c, p. 9).

Watson and Watson-Franke (1985) suggest there are important considerations when gathering and analyzing life-history data. Researchers, they maintain, want to know the answers to many questions about the methods used to gather life histories. Some of these questions explore the relationship between the reader/researcher and the writer, the circumstances in which the writer composed the life history, the incentives and motivations to write, the writer's response to the task of compiling the account, and the particular kinds of questions used to elicit the writing. These considerations illuminate several issues that are essential for facilitating the professional development of preservice teachers.

The intent of such questions asked of researchers foreshadows the concerns usefully kept in the forefront of my thinking as I develop and maintain productive relationships with individuals who reveal their innermost feelings, including their fears, frustrations and fantasies, about the connections between their past experiences of schools, classrooms and teachers and their prospective professional lives: 1) the trustworthiness of the reader of life histories must be assured and open communication must be sought; 2) while there is clearly a hierarchical relationship between prospective teachers and their teacher, that differential must be minimized; 3) while incentives and motivations for writing may be external and, as a result, induce the written account to be cast in particular molds, the most productive life-history accounts are developed when writers are intrinsically motivated and take advantage of the opportunity to make meaning of their prior education-related experiences; 4) some students of teaching will require considerable urging to complete the task while others will tackle it without question; and, 5) the kinds of structures provided for developing the organization and substance of the written account profoundly affect the final product, as do the particular kinds of questions and topics suggested.

Responding to Life-History Accounts: Continuing the Conversation through Dialogue Journal Writing

Insights gained from writing a personal history account provide starting points for further and deeper examination. The dialogue journal offers one vehicle and forum for entering and continuing the conversation begun in the life-history account. The use of dialogue journals in preservice teacher education, in association with constructed and shared life-history accounts, I maintain, promotes elements of reflection (see Knowles, 1991b; Martin, 1991) — although this is a point we need to be cautious about — and the development of new perspectives (Bolin, 1988; see also Staton, 1987). A dialogue in journal format, as opposed to a face-to-face interaction, enhances the opportunities for critically reviewing the origins of a teacher's thinking. By critically reviewing I mean, in Apple's (1975) terms, 'radically reexamining ... current positions and asking potential questions about the relationship that exists between these positions and the social structures from which they arise' (p. 127). Through the reflexive practices of writing and dialogue both the thinking and the contexts in which the constructs were developed are laid bare.

There are three main rationales for using dialogue journals. First, there are strengths in teacher educators and preservice teachers developing close working relationships and this occurs when each are immersed in the other's development and learnings. Mentorship is both a powerful role-modelling technique and a more direct way to share new and established under-standings of classrooms and schools (e.g. see Bey and Holmes, 1990; Shul-man and Colbert, 1987). When learners and teachers are in synchronous relationships — when they begin to have shared understandings about the world of teaching, and subsequently develop common goals and inquiries — the potential to influence each other is heightened (see e.g. Bullough and Gitlin, 1989; Witherell and Makler, 1989).

Second, intensive dialogical interactions serve an assessment function. The weaknesses and strengths of prospective teachers may more readily come to the fore, enabling purposeful individualized attention to experi-enced difficulties (see Bullough and Gitlin, 1989). Commentaries by writers who trust readers are likely to portray difficult events and problems, import-ant for avoiding 'mis-educative experiences' (Dewey, 1938). This element of dialogue journal writing presents a formative evaluation strategy that is particularly useful during field placements and practice/student teaching, when there are limited opportunities for face-to-face contact.

Third, professors of teacher education, like the preservice teachers under their tutelage, have their own scripts, or internal dialogues, about learning to teach and working in classrooms (Knowles, 1990; Knowles and Holt-Reynolds, 1991). These separate narratives, the instructor's and the preservice teachers', seldom meeting with synergetic force. Dialogue journal writing has qualities which show great promise and potential to significantly aid in productive exchanges and understandings of their separate scripts (Knowles, 1990).

In other places (see Knowles, 1991b, 1990; Knowles and Holt-Reynolds, 1991) I have made explicit other purposes and arguments for the use of dialogue journals. For example, helping preservice teachers make their implicit beliefs about teaching known is of central importance, as is the very act of listening to their internal narratives.

Considerable emotional investment and time commitment are neces-sary, however, if one is to become intensely involved in responding to dialogue journal writing in a manner that proves satisfying for both the reader and writer. When both reader and writer gain in knowledge and understanding from the experience, transformational power is offered to both individuals (see Bullough and Gitlin, 1989; Witherell and Makler, 1989). One key to achieving this is limiting the numbers of preservice teachers for which a professor, or other co-instructors, are responsible —

groups of less than ten may be the most productive number for mentors/ journal readers to handle.

Thus, a combination of writing life-history accounts and dialogue journal writing has been most productive in my teaching. Both vehicles tend to provide many opportunities for reflection, in Kathryn's words: 'to test the waters (and their source) . . . of our beliefs and thinking about teaching, putting everything in a more constructive framework.' In that way writing life-history accounts and conversing in dialogue journals helps set the scene for reflective practice opportunities — indeed they represent elements of reflective practice in both the past and the present.

Life-History Accounts as Mirrors: Towards Conceptualizing Reflection

By drawing on the work of others, in this brief section I discuss aspects of the notion of reflection — I use the term reflexive inquiry and reflexive practices synonymously. First I briefly explore the value and purpose of reflection. Second, I suggest some definitional elements of reflection and, third, I outline some basic assumptions about reflection. Fourth, I discuss some of the orientations and characteristics of reflection which lead almost full circle into, fifth, the place of reflexive inquiry in teacher education.

Value and Purpose

In thinking about reflection within the context of preservice teacher education, a fundamental question needs to be answered: Why is it useful and important for teachers to engage in reflection? Because schools and society are constantly changing, the argument is often made that teachers need to be reflective in order to cope effectively with changing circumstances (Schön, 1983). Further, teacher education programs can rarely prepare teachers to be effective in all kinds of classroom situations (Grant and Zeichner, 1984), and teachers need ways to familiarize themselves with ways of acting that induces ongoing professional development and renewal. Given that the pedagogical knowledge base in teacher education has been criticized as being inconsistent and unorganized, and that field experiences in classrooms — including student/practice teaching — are seen as replicating the status quo: 'reflection is valued because it interrupts the smooth flow of events' (Floden and Buchmann, 1990, p. 53). It effectively challenges the thinking about events, circumstances, and philosophies which constitute and value the status quo.

Reflection, to extend its purpose further, is seen as a means of emancipation and empowerment, a vehicle for allowing both teacher educators and teachers to take control of environments and circumstances in which they work and students learn (Connelly and Clandinin, 1988; Noffke and Brennan, 1988; Wildman and Niles, 1987). While a radical critique of schooling emphasizes the school's role in preserving social inequities, the progressive social vision puts faith in the power of education to shape a new social order that truly plays out the democratic role of schooling. Reflection is seen as one way of re-socialization, which is deemed necessary: 'especially if new ways of teaching are to be fostered' (Feiman-Nemser, 1990, p. 227).

There is a strong sense of morality associated with the reflective teacher (e.g. Liston and Zeichner, 1987). It is assumed that acts of reflection will lead to 'moral', 'correct', and 'ethical' choices; however, when Dewey (1933) defined reflective action 'as behavior which involves active, persistent and careful consideration of any belief or practice in light of the grounds that support it and the further consequences to which it leads' (Grant and Zeichner, 1984, p. 4) he believed that the attitudes of open-mindedness, responsibility and wholeheartedness were prerequisites for suitable reflective action (see also Chapter 2). Open-mindedness refers to attention to all the possible alternatives, responsibility involves the careful consideration of the consequences to which an action leads, and wholeheartedness refers to the fact that open-mindedness and responsibility are central in the life of the reflective teacher (Grant and Zeichner, 1984).

Reflection Defined

While there are varied definitions of reflection (see e.g. Dewey, 1933; Grimmet and Erickson, 1988; Schön, 1983, 1987; Van Manen, 1977) and as many orientations towards reflective practice — for example, personal, technical, practical and critical (Weiss and Louden, 1989) — the underlying theme running through these definitions is that reflection is an intra-personal process (Canning, 1990) through which personal and professional knowing can occur (Sikes and Aspinwall, 1990). Reflection is seen as a process and method of informing practice with reason (Liston and Zeichner, 1987; Schön, 1988; Witherell and Makler, 1989). Reflection is *not* seen as being static; implicit in its meaning is action (Schön, 1983; Noffke and Brennan, 1988). It is seen as a vehicle for promoting changed behaviors and practices (Boyd and Fales, 1983), and a means of improving foresight (Buchmann, 1990; Schön, 1983), lessening the chances of taking inappropriate lines of action.

Basic Assumptions

There are some basic assumptions associated with reflexive inquiry. The first assumption is that reflection does lead to better action (Noffke and Brennan, 1988; Schön, 1983); another, is that it is necessary to reflect in order to be an effective teacher (Grant and Zeichner, 1984). The opposing view suggests that effective teachers act primarily on intuition, spontaneously rather than reflectively. Grant and Zeichner (1984) suggest, however, that teachers who are described as effective may act spontaneously and intuitively but reflect prior to and after their actions. To reflect during action is more difficult. These views mirror Schön's (1983) position.

Another assumption underlying the concept of reflection is that multiple ways of seeing persist during the teaching act (Valli and Taylor, 1989). This assumption holds true when viewed from Dewey's (1933) perspective, given the implicit link between reflection and action through reflective teaching. For Dewey, reflection is a practical activity embedded in the act of teaching (Noffke and Brennan, 1988). Writing journals and other autobiographical texts, doing action-research, debriefing after practice, and peer/supervisor support groups have increasingly been advocated as ways in which reflection can be facilitated (e.g. Butt, Raymond and Yamagishi, 1988; Charvoz, Crow and Knowles, 1988; Cooper, 1989; Gore and Zeichner, 1990; Knowles, 1991b; Martin, 1991; Yinger and Clark, 1981).

Orientations and Characteristics

Reflection is conceptualized through varied orientations and hierarchies of teacher education programs (e.g. Boyd and Fales, 1983; Canning, 1990; Kemmis, 1985; Noffke and Brennan, 1988; Schön, 1988). Some of the more common orientations include the technological, practical/problematic, personal and critical (see also Chapter 1). These different frameworks presume different interests (Weiss and Louden, 1989). *Technological reflection* considers choices centered on economy, efficiency and effectiveness of working in classrooms. *Practical/problematic reflection* is concerned with the 'resolution of problems in action' which occur within the regular contexts of teaching, yet defy easy, routine solutions. *Personal reflection* considers the interpretations of personal meanings, assumptions and judgments when making decisions. *Critical reflection* considers the political, ethical and social contexts questioning the taken-for-granted conceptions of teachers' work, and the striving towards construction of educational communities based on democratic ideals (see van Manen, 1987; Noffke and Brennan, 1988).

Hierarchically, critical reflection is predominantly viewed as a higher level of thinking than technological, personal and practical/problematic reflection (e.g. van Manen, 1977). Biermann, Mintz and McCullough (1988) identify three hierarchical levels of reflection among students of teaching. The first level is likened to the metaphor of production where teachers are technologically capable. They possess basic teaching skills and the technical ability to convey knowledge; however, they tend to perpetuate the models of teaching they have experienced and are primarily concerned with outcomes of instruction rather than processes. The second level of reflection is the decision-making level and is likened to the metaphor of choice. Teachers at this level possess and use first-level skills but also practice appropriate, consistent and defensible instructional decision-making. They emphasize problem-solving and critical thinking, make thoughtful choices, assess the various consequences of instruction, show commitment to continued personal growth, and are tolerant of individual differences in students. The metaphor of liberation is used with the third level of reflection. A teacher at this level strives to continue a program of self-directed growth, applies moral and ethical criteria to educational decisions, assumes personal responsibility, provides leadership, resolves inconsistencies between beliefs, values and behaviours through reflection, and experiments and takes risks.

Noffke and Brennan (1988) caution against hierarchical models of thinking about reflection and view reflection as a relational process, not a linear one. They conceptualize an alternative model in which reflection is a 'dynamic, multi-dimensional, and social activity' (p. 24). Their model is built on dimensions, not hierarchies and layers. There is no 'more is better' reflection, but all dimensions are important for the process. One plane of the figure, the sensory dimension, is occupied by the actors in the social world — their material reality, skills and actions. The second dimension consists of ideals which connote a reference to moral and ethical principles such as caring, justice and equality. The historical dimension looks at how educational practices evolved and came to be developed. The 'determinants' dimension of the model depicts the structures of the cultural, political and economic spheres as they intersect with class, gender and race dynamics.

Schön (1988) conceptualized reflective teaching as 'giving reason'. For Schön, reflection is comprised of 'reflection-in-action' and 'reflection-on-action'. Reflection-in-action is 'reflection on phenomena, and on one's spontaneous ways of thinking and acting, undertaken in the midst of action to guide further action' (Schön, 1988, p. 22); reflection-on-action consists of reflection after the event, and reflection *on* reflection-in-action. Shulman (1988) cautions against viewing reflection in the form of dichotomies because the teaching world does not divide readily into extreme groups. Also cautioned is the view that 'school knowledge or technical rationality "leave no room" for certain more reflective, artistic or responsive processes' (Shulman, 1988, p. 33). It is important to combine the technical and the reflective, the theoretical and the practical, and the universal and the concrete. Shulman maintains that while it is important to 'give reason', it is also important to 'marry' those reasons to what is reasonable (see also Chapter 2).

The personal orientation is conceptualized by Boyd and Fales (1983). They define reflection as 'the process of creating and clarifying the meaning of experience in terms of self (self in relation to self and self in relation to the world) where the outcome is a changed conceptual perspective' (p. 101). They describe reflection as composed of six stages: 1) a sense of inner discomfort; 2) identification or clarification of the concern; 3) openness to new information from internal and external sources, with the ability to observe and take in a variety of perspectives; 4) resolution, expressed as 'integration', 'coming together', 'acceptance of self-reality', and 'creative synthesis'; 5) establishing continuity of self with past, present and future; and, 6) deciding whether to act on the outcome of the reflective process (p. 106). These observations serve well my thinking about reflection for they replicate the kinds of steps through which writers of personal history accounts move. Kathryn's case, mentioned earlier, serves as a good example of this reflective process.

Kemmis (1985), however, believes that reflection is a political act, one which is action-oriented and embedded in history. It is a social process that serves human interests and a powerful vehicle to reconstruct social life. It shapes ideology and in turn is shaped by ideology. It needs to simultaneously explore both thought and action, and the individual and society. Further, according to Kemmis (1985), research about reflection needs to be reflective; individuals and groups must engage in 'ideology-critique and participatory, collaborative and emancipatory action research' (Noffke and Brennan, 1988, p. 16).

Reflection in Teacher Education

Zeichner and Teitelbaum (1982) argue that a critical inquiry approach to student teaching is ethically more justifiable than a personalized approach. A teacher education program constructed along the lines of a personalized approach is built in accordance with the needs of education students and 'an attempt is made to have the substance of the program address questions that students are asking at their present level of development' (pp. 95–96). According to them, the survival-oriented (personalized) approach, which 'assumes that current concerns must be resolved before more mature concerns can emerge' (p. 98), does not allow for thoughtful and reflective teaching.

While the critical inquiry orientation is often described as including all the other orientations, and so is all encompassing in one respect, I think the same case can be made for the personal orientation. While examining personal beliefs, values and orientations first, the need to examine them in the socio-political context arises (Sikes and Aspinwall, 1990). Thus, the critical inquiry approach can be viewed as a top-down approach, and the personal orientation can be viewed as a bottom-up approach.

Canning (1990) describes a personal orientation that begins as survival oriented and builds up to self-realization. She conceptualizes reflection as a process characterized by rambling, internal dialogue, questioning and the achievement of insight. She categorized reflection into two major categories: 1) those examples in which the person reflecting was focusing only on things outside him/herself (i.e. classroom events, students, and principles of learning and teaching); and, 2) those examples in which the person reflecting was including him/herself as an object of reflection, demonstrating acceptance of self and a clarity of self perception.

Learning the Discourse of Reflection:
From Life Histories to Reflexive Practice

I have presented the various perspectives on reflexive inquiry as a way of driving home the multi-faceted nature of the concept. Hopefully, I have also made it clear in the previous sections that students of teaching bring valuable insights — although not necessarily always the most substantiated and sound — to the arena of their new-found profession. My view is that these aspects of their thinking are wonderful and opportunistic springboards for professional development that is linked with not only the concept of life-history accounts but also with the more broadly identified issues and dilemmas in teacher education.

That most prospective teachers find it difficult to consider in critical ways the socio-political contexts of their future work world may merely reflect their inexperience at testing many of the assumptions about the world of teaching from other than their personal perspectives. It has been documented that only few teachers in preparation reflect critically in the socio-political context. Most use personal orientations (e.g. Gore and Zeichner, 1990). Individuals start with themselves when reflecting before encompassing the social, economic and political contexts. And, indeed, this seems like a logical place for individuals to start, and it belies the insistence that reflection is developmental in nature. It implies the position that the best place to start the practice, and the habitual use of it, is to begin with aspects of teaching that are more personal and immediately relevant, or seen to be relevant. The familiar is more comfortable than the unfamiliar as a place to *start* the process.

Further, it may not be reasonable to expect great evidence of critical reflection in prospective teachers within the time frame of typical teacher preparation programs. It may be more helpful first to adopt a more personal orientation in the advocacy of reflexive inquiry and *then* build on to it the characteristics of critical inquiry — and this is the essential element of a conceptualization of reflection in which life-history analysis is a mirror. This position withstanding, I take the view that many prospective teachers have already developed notions and practices akin to reflection and the formalization of reflexive inquiry through the construction of the life-history accounts and the dialogue journal writing merely taps into informal well established evaluative/assessment practices of preservice teachers. The importance of mentioning the various orientations to and characteristics of reflection then, is to suggest that there are indeed multiple ways in which potential teachers may explore their own preconceptions and pre-intentions about teaching, in the process having their internal dialogues and practical arguments challenged, and new thinking put in place.

To present linear conceptions of reflection is problematic, as are developmental constructs. While my preference is ultimately to seek the development of reflexive inquiry in the vein of Grant and Zeichner's (1984) stance, considering the socio-political influences, the enhancement of the developing practices of new teachers may be more usefully served by maintaining a broad front of challenges to long-standing beliefs about practice that explorations of pertinent life-history accounts may present.

The process of cultivating reflexive practices is, in the end, both a vehicle and catalyst for professional development. It is an avenue to induce, in prospective and beginning teachers, alternative approaches to thinking about practice, about the relationships between cause and effect of those practices, and about the place of those practices within the communities of classroom, school and society. The construction and use of life-history accounts in preservice teacher education provide opportunities for preservice teachers to learn from both the process and substance of their engagement in reflexive practical inquiry. And, this is but one avenue for the conceptualization of reflection in teacher education.

Acknowledgments

Rosebud Elijah provided unswerving support in my recent writing endeavours. She assisted with the preparation of the literature for the section of the paper which defines 'reflection' and reviewed a much earlier draft of the whole manuscript. Thanks also to Ardra L. Cole for her thoughtful critique of later drafts of the manuscript and for her insightful suggestions that propelled this revision.

References

ALLPORT, G. (1942) *The use of personal documents in psychological science*, New York, NY: Social Science Research Council.

APPLE, M. (1975) 'Scientific interests and the nature of educational institutions', in PINAR, W. (ed.) *Curriculum theorizing*, Berkeley, CA: McCutcheon, pp. 120–30.

BALL, S.J. and GOODSON, I.F. (1984) 'Introduction: Defining the curriculum; histories and ethnographies', in GOODSON, I.F. and BALL, S.J. (eds) *Defining the curriculum: Histories and ethnographies*, London, UK: The Falmer Press, pp. 1–14.

BECKER, H. (1952) 'The career of the Chicago school teacher', in HAMMERSLEY, M. and WOODS, P. (eds) *The process of schooling*, London, UK: Routledge and Kegan Paul.

— (1966) 'Introduction', in SHAW, C.L. *The jack roller: A delinquent boy's own story*, Chicago, IL: University of Chicago Press, pp. v–xviii.

BERTAUX, D. (1981) 'From the life-history approach to the transformation of sociological practice', in BERTAUX, D. (ed.) *Biography and society: The life-history approach in the social sciences*, Newberry Park, CA: Sage, pp. 29–45.

BEY, T.M. and HOLMES, C.T. (eds) (1990) *Mentoring: Developing successful new teachers*, Reston, VA: Association of Teacher Educators.

BEYNON, J. (1985) 'Institutional change and career histories in a comprehensive school', in BALL, S.J. and GOODSON, I.F. (eds) *Teachers' lives and careers*, London, UK: The Falmer Press, pp. 158–79.

BIERMANN, M.J., MINTZ, S.L. and McCULLOUGH, L.L. (1988) 'Reflection in the University of Virginia's five-year teacher education program', unpublished manuscript, University of Virginia, Charlottesville, VA.

BOGDAN, R. and TAYLOR, S. (1970) *Introduction to qualitative research methods*, London, UK: Wiley.

BOLIN, F.S. (1988) 'Helping student teachers think about teaching', *Journal of Teacher Education*, **39**(2), pp. 48–54.

BOYD, E. and FALES, A.W. (1983) 'Reflective learning: Key to learning from experience', *Journal of Humanistic Psychology*, **23**(2), pp. 99–117.

BUCHMANN, M. (1990) 'Beyond the lonely choosing will: Professional development in teacher thinking', *Teachers College Record*, **91**(4), pp. 481–508.

BULLOUGH, R.V. Jr. and GITLIN, A.D. (1989) 'Toward educative communities: Teacher education and the quest for the reflective practitioner', *Qualitative Studies in Education*, **2**(4), pp. 285–98.

BUTT, R., RAYMOND, D. and YAMAGISHI, L. (1988, April) *Autobiographic praxis: Studying the formation of teachers' knowledge*, paper presented at the annual meeting of the American Educational Research Association, New Orleans, LA.

CANNING, C. (1990, April) *Reflection: Out on a limb. An intrapersonal process and the development of voice*, paper presented at the annual meeting of the American Educational Research Association, Boston, MA.

CHARVOZ, A., CROW, N.A. and KNOWLES, J.G. (1988, April) *A case study of journal writing: Is it a useful tool for enhancing reflection in preservice teachers?* paper presented at the annual meeting of the American Educational Research Association, New Orleans, LA.

CONNELLY, F.M. and CLANDININ, D.J. (1988) *Teachers as curriculum planners: narratives of experience*, New York, NY: Teachers College Press.

COOPER, J.E. (1989, March) *Telling our own stories: The process of journal writing*, paper presented at the annual meeting of the American Educational Research Association, San Francisco, CA.

DENZIN, N.K. (1989) *Interpretive biography*, Newbury Park, CA: Sage Publications.

DEWEY, J. (1933) *Education and experience*, New York, NY: Macmillan Publishing Co., Inc.

— (1933). *How we think: A restatement of the relation of reflective thinking to the educative process*, Boston, MA: D.C. Heath.

DOLLARD, J. (1949) *Criteria for the life history*, New Haven, CT: Yale University Press.

DYK, W. (1938) *Son of old man hat: A Navajo autobiography*, New York, NY: Harcourt, Brace.

FARADAY, A. and PLUMMER, K. (1979) 'Doing life histories', *Sociological Review*, **27**(4), pp. 773–93.

FEIMAN-NEMSER, S. (1990) 'Teacher preparation: Structural and conceptual alternatives', in HOUSTON, W.R. (ed.) *Handbook of research on teacher education*, New York: Macmillan Publishing Co., pp. 212–33.

FLODEN, R.E. and BUCHMANN, M. (1990) 'Philosophical inquiry in teacher education', in HOUSTON, W.R. (ed.) *Handbook of research on teacher education*, New York: Macmillan Publishing Co., pp. 42–58.

FREEMAN, J.M. (1979) *Untouchables: An Indian life history*, Stanford, CA: Stanford University Press.

GOODSON, I.F. (1991) 'Teachers lives in educational research', in GOODSON, I.F. and WALKER, R. (eds) *Biography, identity and schooling: Episodes in educational research*, London, UK: The Falmer Press, pp. 137–40.

— (1983) 'The use of life histories in the study of teaching', in HAMMERSLEY, M. (ed.) *The ethnography of schooling*, Driffield, UK: Nafferton.

— (1981) 'Life histories and the study of schooling', *Interchange*, **11**(4).

GOODSON, I.F. and COLE, A.L. (1991, October) *Exploring the teachers' professional knowledge: Constructing identity and community*, paper presented at the Spencer Hall Invitational Conference on Teacher Development, University of Western Ontario, London, Ontario, Canada.

GORE, J.M. and ZEICHNER, K.M. (1990) 'Action research and reflective teaching in preservice teacher education: A case study from the United States', in STEVENSON, R.B. and NOFFKE, S.E. (eds) *Action research and teacher education: International perspectives*, (Special Studies in Teaching and Teacher Education, No. 4), Buffalo, NY: Graduate School of Education Publications, Buffalo Research Institute on Education for Teaching, State University of New York at Buffalo.

GRANT, C.A. and ZEICHNER, K.M. (1984) 'On becoming a reflective teacher', in GRANT, C.A. (ed.) *Preparing for reflective teaching*, Boston, MA: Allyn & Bacon, Inc., pp. 1–18.

GRIMMET, P. and ERICKSON, G. (eds) (1988) *Reflection in teacher education*, New York: Teachers College Press.

HOLT-REYNOLDS, D. (1990, October) *Entering preservice teachers' internal dialogues: The power of reflection to shape practical arguments*, (Part 2 of symposium: Changing the discourse of reflection). A paper presented at the Twelfth Conference on Curriculum Theory and Classroom Practice, The Bergamo Center, Dayton, OH.

KEMMIS, S. (1985) 'Action research and the politics of reflection', in BOUD, D., KEOGH, R. and WALKER, D. (eds) *Reflection: Turning experience into learning*, London, UK: Kogan Page, pp. 139–63.

KNOWLES, J.G. (1989a) 'Beginning teachers biographies and coping strategies: An exploratory case study', unpublished dissertation, University of Utah, Salt Lake City, UT.

— (1989b) 'Parents' rationales and teaching methods for home schooling: The role of biography', *Education and Urban Society*, **21**(1), pp. 69–84.

— (1989c) 'Teaching in the elementary school/practicum in teaching methods (Education 406/307, Fall Term, 1989', unpublished course outline, School of Education, The University of Michigan, Ann Arbor, MI.

— (1990, October) *Entering preservice teachers' internal dialogues: the power of reflection to shape practice* (Part 2 of symposium: Changing the discourse of reflection), a paper presented at the Twelfth Conference on Curriculum Theory and Classroom Practice, The Bergamo Center, Dayton, OH.

— (1991a) 'Parents' rationales for operating home schools', *Journal of Contemporary Ethnography*, **20**(2).

— (1991b, February) *Journal use in preservice teacher education: A personal and reflexive response to comparison and criticisms*, a paper presented at the Annual Meeting of the Association of Teacher Educators, New Orleans, LA.

— (1992) 'Models for understanding preservice and beginning teachers' biographies: Illustrations from case studies', in GOODSON, I.F. (ed.) *Studying teachers' lives*, London, UK: Routledge.

KNOWLES, J.G. and HOEFLER, V.B. (1989) 'The student teacher who wouldn't go away: Learning from failure', *Journal of Experiential Education*, **12**(2), pp. 29–41.

KNOWLES, J.G. and HOLT-REYNOLDS, D. (1991) 'The convergence of teacher educators' and preservice teachers' personal histories: Shaping pedagogy', *Teachers College Record*, **93**(1), pp. 87–113.

LANGNESS, L.L. and FRANK, G. (1981) *An anthropological approach to biography*, Novato, CA: Chandler and Sharp.

LISTON, D.P. and ZEICHNER, K.M. (1987) Reflective teacher education and moral deliberation, *Journal of Teacher Education*, **2–8**.

LORTIE, D. (1975) *Schoolteacher: A sociological study*, Chicago, IL: University of Chicago Press.

MARTIN, B.J. (1991, February) *Journal use in preservice teacher education: Reflection, dialogue, and cognitive change*, a paper presented at the Annual Meeting of the Association of Teacher Educators, New Orleans, LA.

MEYERHOFF, B. (1982) 'Life history among the elderly: Performance, visibility, and re-membering', in RUBY, J. (ed.) *A crack in the mirror: Reflexive practices in anthro-pology*, Philadelphia, PA: University of Pennsylvania Press, pp. 99–117.

NOFFKE, S.E. and BRENNAN, M. (April, 1988) *The dimensions of reflection: A concep-tual and contextual analysis*, a paper presented at the annual meeting of the American Educational Research Association, New Orleans.

PILLEMER, D.B. (1984) 'Flashbulb memories of the assassination attempt on President Reagan', *Cognition*, **16**, pp. 63–80.

PILLEMER, D.B., GOLDSMITH, L.R., PANTER, A.T. and WHITE, S.H. (1988) 'Very long-term memories of the first year in college', *Journal of Experimental Psychology: Learning, Memory, and Cognition*, **144**, pp. 709–15.

RADIN, P. (1926) *Crashing Thunder: The autobiography of an American Indian*, New York, NY: Appleton.

SCHÖN, D.A. (1983) *The reflective practitioner: How professionals think in action*, New York, NY: Basic Books.

— (1987) *Educating the reflective practitioner*, San Francisco: Jossey-Bass.

— (1988) 'Coaching reflective teaching', in GRIMMETT, P. and ERICKSON, G. (eds) *Reflec-tion in teacher education*, New York, NY: Teachers College Press, pp. 19–30.

SHAW, C.R. (1966) *The jack roller: A delinquent boy's own story*, Chicago, IL: Univer-sity of Chicago Press.

SHOSTAK, M. (1981) *Nisa: The Life and words of a !Kung woman*, Cambridge, MA: Harvard University Press.

SHULMAN, J.H. and COLBERT, J.A. (eds) (1987) *Mentor teacher casebook*, San Fran-cisco, CA: Far West Laboratory for Educational Research and Development.

SHULMAN, L.S. (1988) 'The dangers of dichotomous thinking in education', in GRIMMETT, P. and ERICKSON, G. (eds) *Reflection in teacher education*, New York, NY: Teachers College Press, pp. 31–8.

SIKES, P. and ASPINWALL, K. (1990, April) *Time to reflect: Biographical study, personal insight and professional development*, a paper presented at the Annual Meeting of the American Educational Research Association, Boston, MA.

SIMMONS, L. (ed.) (1949) *Sun Chief: The autobiography of a Hopi Indian*, New Haven, CT: Yale University Press.

SMITH, L.M., DWYER, D.C., PRUNTY, J.J. and KLEINE, P.F. (1988) *Innovation and change in schooling: History, politics, and agency* (Book 3, Anatomy of educational innovation: A mid to long term re-study and reconstructural), London, UK: The Falmer Press.

STATON, J. (1987) 'The power of responding to dialogue journals', in FULWILER, T. (ed.) *The Journal Book*, Portsmouth, NH: Boynton/ Cook Publishers, pp. 47–63.

VALLI, L. and TAYLOR, N. (1989, April) 'Evaluating a reflective teacher education model', in *Issues of reflection in teacher education research and practice*. Symposium conducted at the annual meeting of the American Educational Research Association, San Francisco, CA.

VAN MANEN, M. (1989) *Researching lived experience*, London, Ontario: Althouse Press.

— (1977) 'Linking ways of knowing with ways of being practical', *Curriculum Inquiry*, **6**(3), pp. 205–28.

WATSON, L.C. and WATSON-FRANKE, M-B. (1985) 'Interpreting life histories: An anthropological inquiry', New Brunswick, NJ: Rutgers University Press.

WEISS, J. and LOUDEN, W. (1989) *Images of reflection*, Perth, Australia: The Ontario Institute for Studies in Education (Toronto, Ontario, Canada) and The Ministry of Education, Western Australia.

WHITE, R.T. (1982) 'Memory for personal events', *Human Learning*, **1**, pp. 171–83.

WILDMAN, T.M. and NILES, J.A. (1987) 'Reflective teachers: Tensions between abstractions and realities', *Journal of Teacher Education*, **28**(4), pp. 25–31.

WILEY, N. (1986) 'Early American sociology and "The Polish Peasant"', *Sociological Theory*, **4**, pp. 20–40.

WITHERELL, C. and MAKLER, A. (1989, March) *Giving each other reason: Building a community of inquirers through collaborative teacher education*, a paper presented at the annual meeting of the American Educational Research Association, San Francisco, CA.

WITHERALL, C. and NODDINGS, N. (1991) 'Prologue: An invitation to our readers', in WITHERALL, C. and NODDING, N. (eds) *Stories lives tell: Narrative and dialogue in education*, New York, NY: Teachers College Press.

WOODS, P. (1984) 'Teacher, self and curriculum', in GOODSON, L.F. and BALL, S.J. (eds) *Defining the curriculum: Histories and ethnographies*, London, UK: The Falmer Press, pp. 1–14.

YINGER, R.J. and CLARK, C.M. (1981) *Reflective journal writing: Theory and practice* (Occasional Paper No. 50), East Lansing, MI: Michigan State University, Institute for Research on Teaching.

ZEICHNER, K.M. and TEITELBAUM, K. (1982) 'Personalized and inquiry-oriented teacher education: An analysis of two approaches to the development of curriculum for field-based experiences', *Journal of Education for Teaching*, **8**, pp. 95–117.

6 Tutors' Professional Knowledge of Supervision and the Implications for Supervision Practice

K. Anne Proctor

There are two main tasks for teacher educators who are concerned to promote reflection in teaching. The first of these is to decide what reflective teaching is, and the second is to decide how to promote reflective teaching at different stages of professional development. Clearly these two aspects are inextricably related, but still it is possible to given emphasis to one or the other at any one time. In this chapter the emphasis is on the latter, focusing in particular on the role of supervision of student teaching in enhancing reflective teaching. Some findings from an extended study of supervision practice are described and applied to the task of developing reflective practice.

Reflection in Teaching

One aspect of reflection is evaluation, described by Shavelson and Stern (1981, p. 471) as a 'phase of teaching whereby teachers assess their plans and accomplishments and so revise them for the future'. Lowyck (1986) points to the importance of personal information processing activities, which come after teaching and appear to contribute to the development of professional knowledge. A further dimension comes from the work of Grant and Zeichner (1984), who, by referring to the ongoing nature of reflection, move away from the idea that it comes only after teaching, rather than being part of the preparation and implementation of teaching as well. They also emphasize the responsibility of the teacher to improve practice in the interest of pupils.

In summary, reflective teaching can be seen as associated with the following:

- looking back in a critical way on what has already taken place;
- building up a body of professional knowledge, related to technical, strategic and ethical aspects of teaching;
- using this body of knowledge in a critical way in new situations;
- widening the range of criteria which will influence the reflective/ critical process;
- building up a personal set of criteria as a result of the reflective/ critical process.

The purpose in this chapter is to examine the role of supervising tutors in encouraging a reflective approach in student teachers practising teaching.

Promoting Reflective Practice

In attempts to help tutors to become more effective, various approaches to supervision practice have been advocated. Micro-teaching draws on a skill-based approach, which is based on the assumption that certain teaching skills which are believed to be effective can be taught to teachers and student teachers by a process of explanation, modelling, practice and suitable feed-back (e.g. Griffiths, 1974; Heath and Neilson, 1974; Shanker, 1974). This approach can be criticized on the grounds that: it is mechanistic; it cannot encourage a reflective attitude; it cannot do justice to the way teachers build up their professional knowledge of teaching and the personal way in which skills are applied in a specific classroom situation.

It is argued, instead, that student teachers will benefit from sharing the professional knowledge of experienced teachers in the classroom (Brown et al., 1988; Soloman, 1987; McNamara and Desforges, 1978). This is not easy to achieve but McAlpine et al. (1988) have had some degree of success. At the same time student teachers should not depend on following the dictates of experienced teachers if they are to develop their own practice in an autonomous and reflective way. It is suggested that this is most likely to be achieved by the practice of a clinical approach to supervision with its emphasis on the autonomy of the teacher or student teacher in deciding on issues for discussion (Cogan, 1976; Goldhammer, 1969; Turney et al., 1982). The co-operative discursive approach described by Ashton et al. (1983) and associated with the IT-INSET movement (Initial Training and the Inservice Education of Teachers) seems to offer the potential for sharing professional knowledge as well as reflecting on that knowledge.

While accepting the validity of the clinical approach to supervision, Stones (1984) believes that student teachers cannot be in a position to exercise autonomy if they have not been introduced to relevant theory about the way people learn and are motivated to learn. He advocates a model of supervision which encourages an analytical, theoretically-based approach which encourages the application of psychopedagogical theory to the planning for learning and the evaluation of teaching.

Studies which have compared supervisors' accounts of what they say they do with what they actually do, have found anomalies between the two (Terrell *et al.*, 1985; Gitlin *et al.*, 1985; Mansfield, 1986; Zeichner and Tabachnick, 1982) For example, Terrell *et al.* (1985) found that supervisors who advocated group activities in the classroom, in fact spent their time giving attention to class teaching. According to the reports of Mansfield (1986) tutors' analysis of the teaching of student teachers did not improve substantially, even when they were made aware of shortcomings in their practice. This being the case, it would appear that they are either rather incompetent or successful in deceiving themselves. A further example is described by Zeichner and Tabachnick (1982) who found that tutors who believed that they were implementing a clinical approach to supervision were, in fact, practising very different forms of supervision which did not reflect the philosophy of the clinical approach.

These anomalies suggest something more than the need for better training for tutors. They suggest the need for a better understanding of the way tutors operate when they are supervising and, more importantly, the way they make sense of their practice. The study of teaching has been greatly enhanced by in-depth accounts by teachers themselves (Elbaz, 1990). Supervision is another form of teaching and though it has begun to receive much more attention, still it has not benefited from the type of in-depth analysis which classroom teaching has received.

A Study of Supervision Practice

The analysis below draws on data from three studies which have focused on the enterprise of supervision. The first involved one tutor, four teachers and four student teachers, the second, seven tutors, fourteen teachers and fourteen student teachers and the third, fourteen tutors, twenty-six teachers and student teachers. The aim was to examine the process of supervision as it evolved. In order to do this the participants were identified at the beginning of block teaching practices and arrangements were made to consult their views throughout the practice. This was done in a number of ways:

- All the tutors met on a weekly basis for a one hour discussion, which was recorded. The size of the group was never more than seven so that discussion would be informal and easy to sustain.
- The groups were formed at the beginnings of the practices and maintained so that an element of trust would be built up, again to enhance the interaction.
- All the tutors were asked to keep diaries of their activities and to complete summary sheets, on a weekly basis.
- Tutors' teaching notes to students were reviewed regularly.
- All teachers were asked, similarly, to keep diaries.

- All teachers and students were visited at regular intervals so that they could be consulted about the progress of the practice. Detailed written records were kept of these consultations.
- All the teachers and student teachers were involved in final taped discussions at the end of the practice in order to check their views and to give them the opportunity to share their views outside the school situation. Again the group sizes were kept to seven or less with groups of students meeting together and groups of teachers meeting together.

The discussion in the tutor groups centred round four types of questions:

- In general terms what are you looking for when you supervise students on teaching practice?
- What are you looking for when you go into school to see a particular student in a particular classroom?
- What supervision procedures do you normally adopt in classrooms?
- What actually happened when you went into a particular classroom on a particular occasion?

The analysis was based on the discussion which developed round those questions and supported by evidence from all the other sources referred to above.

Influences to Which Tutors Respond in Classrooms

Tutors' understanding of classrooms was very situation specific and it became clear that the only way to access their understanding was by examining their descriptions of what happened on *particular* occasions. What became apparent from the transcription were the qualifications which the tutors applied before they were prepared to make judgments. What they actually noticed in classrooms, what they saw to be significant and what they chose to talk about depended upon what they had come to think about that particular student teacher and the classroom in which that student teacher was placed.

Characteristics of Student Teachers. Tutor 14 summarized, in a typically forthright way, the argument that supervision must be responsive, when she said:

> You couldn't be anything other than be different with different students or the whole thing would be ridiculous wouldn't it!

Before beginning an analysis of tutors' perceptions of student teachers it is essential to make one point very clear. For a majority of the tutors involved it would be wrong to think that they were applying 'labels' to student teachers. Like Hargreaves' (1975) teachers the picture that most tutors built up about the supervisees was very complex despite the limited amount of time which they were able to spend with them. They used their past experience of these student teachers if they already knew them and of other student teachers if they did not. They struggled to find the right words to express what they were trying to say and often their judgments were couched in terms which indicated the process of making a hypothesis which could be proved totally wrong at a later date. If tutors were supervising more than one student teacher they often introduced their initial judgments by describing one student against another.

Moving onto the analysis, a first important perception for tutors was that of the *competence* of the student teacher. However carefully the tutors expressed themselves this judgment of competence or likely competence was being formed quite early on. It was often expressed simply by reference to a 'strong' student or a 'weak' student or a 'very weak' student. Sometimes these judgments were made before the practice started but if the tutors had few pre-conceptions about the student they still began to formulate an approximate judgment of competence quite early on. This often expressed itself in the form of 'there are no worries' or 'everything is all right'.

Tutors also described and responded to student teachers in what may be loosely termed as *personality* factors, e.g.

> ... the student is quite a strong-minded student ... the second student is more of a viable character, more gentle, less inventive.

and, a tutor referring to a teacher and student teacher to show an important aspect of personality said:

> They seem two very different sorts of personality, S is very quiet methodical and gets on with the job and T is vivacious.

An important aspect of student teacher personality for the tutors was *lack of confidence* and it had implications for the tutors' behaviour. If the student teacher was construed as lacking in confidence it nearly always produced an attitude of confidence generation on the part of the tutor.

Another personality characteristic of student teachers which was seen, by tutors, to be significant was the degree to which they were *forthcoming* and prepared to talk to the tutor.

A further student teacher characteristic discussed in some detail by the tutors was the *ability to be self critical*. Some allowed that this may be a skill to be taught but a number talked as if it was a quality of a student's person-ality. These differences were hard to distinguish because tutors often changed their statements when questioned but the importance of the quality was not disputed, only the way it exhibited itself.

Finally, tutors sometimes recognized personality and behavioural characteristics of their student teachers which produced in them a negative reaction,
e.g. Tutor 9:

> It's interesting, you feel a trigger, what did you say? exasperated?
> I've got to be very careful because it arouses in me — I want to prod
> the student to see if anything happens. . . . It doesn't seem to matter
> what I say to the student, she doesn't react — she simply accepts
> whatever I say to her. I think if I was extremely rude and hurtful she
> would sit and accept it. I forbear and it's hard work.

Different from student teacher characteristics were student *beliefs*, but
a tutor's perception of a student teachers' beliefs could have a similarly
important impact on what the tutor expected of the student and hence
required of her/him, e.g.

> What I am really saying is that I think in the case of S1 if I leaned
> (and I would have to do it subtly) I think there might be some prac-
> tice of group work but what I was really saying there, is that I feel
> that basically S1 is not a student who is inclined to believe in the
> value of groups, and I can't honestly see S1, if given a free hand by a
> head teacher two years from now would respond — but if she
> worked for a headteacher who said 'we operate in this way' she
> would toe the line.

This attitude was argued long and hard by that group of tutors. Their argument was important for the indication it gave of the way the supervision
behaviour of some tutors may be *restricted by their expectations about what
could be achieved.*

Judgments about schools and classes. From the earliest weeks of the practice there was evidence from the transcripts of the 'search process' as
tutors began to gather information about the classes in which student
teachers were placed. They picked up aspects of the class which were
likely to have implications for the student, e.g. lack of discipline, pressure
for outcomes, pleasant and supportive atmosphere, potentially difficult
relationships.

The importance of the judgments which were made at that time are
illustrated in the words of Tutor 9 when she was judging whether she would
encourage a student to be innovative:

> . . . and really the decision is made for me on whether I think the
> school will take offence and if I have the least thought that they will
> I wouldn't encourage the student to be very adventurous.

As the practice developed tutors became more explicit about the situation in the school or in the class and at the time they became more explicit about the implications for a particular student teacher. There were both positive and negative examples for the student. For example, on the negative side there were difficulties if: a) in a well organized class it was not easy for a student to have an input which was personal to them; b) a teacher was outgoing and authoritative and a student teacher was reserved and diffident. At the same time a student may have serious difficulties with certain classes because of the behaviour of the class (or the potential behaviour of the class with a different teacher).

Tutors also referred to the positive effects of the school situation. Usually this was the case when the school offered a well organized supportive environment. Even here there could be quite a delicate balance because sometimes the organization could be a threat to a student teacher, perhaps because it was well organized but rigid and/or at odds with the beliefs of the student teacher. Tutors used this information in different ways. At times it was in order to decide about strategies to adopt but at other times it was an excuse for certain things not being able to take place.

The Component Parts of the Tutor's Judgments about Teaching as Related to Supervision Behaviour

The account above shows how tutors reacted to the student teachers they were supervising and the situations in which they were placed. However, it was clear from the tutor discussion that this was not only a reactive process. At the same time tutors drew on ideas of their own about the nature of effective teaching and this conception interacted with their judgments of specific situations. For example, when they found the lack of confidence in a student teacher to be notable this was because lack of confidence was seen to be a quality which would not contribute to effective teaching. Many of these perceptions were shared by a majority of the tutors and indeed the teachers. It was when there were disagreements that it was possible to identify the underlying assumptions because they were raised in discussion.

Taking into account to a greater or lesser extent all or many of the factors outlined above, tutors had to take action (or chose not to take it) in classrooms. Their behaviour was peculiar to themselves but still there was a degree of agreement. The analysis in Figure 6.1 was drawn out of the supervision process as it was taking place. The factors suggested were not explicitly stated as such but were based on evidence from the discussion and checked against subsequent reports. The analysis is presented in the form of a matrix to try and show the relationship between the parts. One side of the matrix refers to what the tutors dealt with and the other to how they dealt with it.

Figure 6.1: Diagram to show the relationship between the component parts of tutors'
judgments about teaching

	What?	
	(a) Efficacy	(b) Tutor's personal focus

		(i) Range
		(ii) Degree of
How?		analysis
		(iii) Confidence
		(iv) Speed

Efficacy Throughout the transcripts there was evidence of tutors' direct
response to things which were happening in the classrooms, e.g. Tutor 8:

> ... the student was doing all kinds of things that you were actually
> itching to tell her about and to offer advice on and I, when I went in,
> I sort of barged in too early and wanted to say all these things to the
> student. . . . I only got through half the things I badly wanted to say.

and: 'Yes, the inadequacies if you like, in that situation stand out — they
jump out and hit you as you walk into the room.'

When things were going very wrong there was almost without exception
an element of *lack of control* on the part of the student. Often this meant
that there was some degree of disorder but even if this was not serious there
was still an element of the class 'running itself'. Discipline and control were
mentioned regularly and consistently throughout the study although it must
be stressed that many tutors did not see control as a discrete element. It was
for this reason that the word efficacy was used to express the concern. Some
examples show this anxiety about efficacy.

> *Tutor 9*: 'the children were milling round, she didn't seem to recognize
> that the children weren't doing what she asked them to do.'
>
> *Tutor 8*: '. . . the children doing inappropriate things, children ungain-
> fully occupied, no attempt by the student to even recognize,
> never mind stamp down on things.'
>
> *Tutor 4*: 'the children are being inattentive, fiddling, disinterested,
> switched off.'

These were illustrations of the situation being out of control but there were
also many examples in which tutors showed that the control situation had
been assessed *before* other matters were taken into consideration, e.g.:

> *Tutor 4*: 'I want to see she is getting some decent work . . . more
> innovative ways of recording or whatever than just taking

the easy way out because actually she's a natural I think. I don't know how she managed so badly on the other practice (i.e. with control) because she really is super with the children.'

i.e. the emphasis on new ways of recording was only appropriate when it was established that control was not a problem.

Tutor 3, in response to a question about what tutors were looking for in a student or classroom, said:

I think that it's going to vary with the student. S's class control relationship with the children is excellent.

i.e. a tutor can begin to look for other things if the control is 'excellent'.

One further example shows how control was not necessarily equated with discipline, although that was a very important part of it in the minds of most tutors.

Tutor 14: 'I'm looking really at his ability to manage the situation . . . not just control the children, he's always been able to do that, but to actually manage their learning.'

Tutor 14 was worried about her student's relationship with the teaching practice situation, i.e. that 'it is happening without his really managing it'. However, even here, her comments show that the aspects of control as discipline were still an important part of her judgment.

Efficacy in the classroom (or rather lack of it) acted as a most important generator of tutor response. Not only did it figure in the accounts of all the tutors but also seemed most of them to be a necessary first hurdle. Tutors did not all see efficacy in the same way and many of them related it to all sorts of other aspects of good and bad teaching but still if there was a lack of overall control in the classroom it became an immediate concern of the tutors. For this reason it merits a place of its own as a crucial aspect of what tutors look for.

Personal focus. Given that the aspect of control did not generate concern, there were other factors which illustrated the knowledge about teaching which tutors used to guide their comments and observations of students. These have been placed under the one heading of 'personal focus' because, despite the fact that they may only be called into operation by a particular situation, still they tended to be tutor specific and they often became apparent in response to more than one student being supervised by a particular tutor. A close scrutiny of the tape transcripts showed certain patterns in the comments of individual tutors.

At its most overt it took the form of a personal teaching skill list, e.g. Tutor 9, being aware of the difficulties of making relevant observations, used a list developed from her own knowledge of important aspects of teaching. The list reflected her psychological background.

Five of the tutors in the sample were particularly associated with one *curriculum* area, i.e. three mathematicians, one scientist and one historian. A further four had a part-time commitment to the language curriculum area. There was evidence of the influence of this on supervision behaviour. It showed itself in a number of ways. First, the initial visit to a student by a curriculum specialist tended to be in the area of her/his curriculum specialism. Secondly, when giving examples of students' work during discussions, tutors would often refer to work in their own specialism. Thirdly, specific advice referring to content or management was offered within their specialism. Finally, to reinforce all this there was an expectation on the part of the teacher and the student that the tutor would show particular interest in her/his own curriculum area.

Apart from curriculum specialism there were other aspects of teaching for which different tutors showed a predisposition. Tutor 5 did not attend the discussion group very often but his supervision notes were available and with the exception of one week for one student he always drew attention to the use of the blackboard and to aspects of class teaching (specifically class question and answer sessions, explanations and the use of visual aids to support explanations and the need to bring the class together to make these explanations), this was to the exclusion of other aspects. The impression that he gave total emphasis to class teaching was reinforced by his comment in private conversation and comment from his students.

One of the characteristics of Tutor 4 was an emphasis on group work (one which she shared with other tutors). She was aware of this and mentioned it on a number of occasions. Tutor 13 referred often to 'match' as one of the things he looked for and his descriptions of what he actually did in classrooms reinforced his statements.

A final illustrative example refers to the development of areas of interest in the classroom and was mentioned frequently by two Early Years tutors, often in conjunction with a reference to first-hand experience and the inadvisability of using any sort of commerical scheme of work. This account includes *illustrations* of personal foci but does not exhaust the number mentioned.

As outlined in Figure 6.1, a truer picture of tutors' knowledge of teaching was gained by considering the ways in which what they looked for might be modified by how they looked for it. The four components which best describe this modification are: i) range, ii) degree of analysis, iii) confidence, iv) speed.

Range.   Range referred to the scope or extent of what the tutor looked for in the classroom, whether applied to aspects of efficacy or aspects characteristic of an individual tutor. When tutors approached classrooms it has been suggested that they were influenced by ill-defined images of what they saw to be good teaching. For different tutors the images could be described as wide or narrow in their scope. This is best illustrated with two contrasting examples. Tutor 4 has been referred to as giving emphasis to group work. This, however, was only one aspect of many to which she gave her attention in different classroom settings. Perhaps a better way of putting that would be to say that she incorporated the group work emphasis into a more general picture of classroom life.

Similarly in approaching the issue of control she defined it very widely to include many aspects of classroom behaviour of student and children. This was apparent in all the tutor discussions and in the notes which she gave to the students. The behaviour and approach of Tutor 5 was in marked contrast to this. His emphasis was on formal class teaching followed by individual written work, and an analysis of his comments and notes to students suggest that these were very narrowly defined. Similarly, control was defined only by the extent to which the student teacher could gain the attention of the children in a class teaching situation. These examples illustrate two extemes and other tutors could be placed at different points along a continuum joining those extremes. This aspect of range also differentiated between specialist curriculum tutors, some of whom were bound by their specialism and others much less so.

Degree of analysis. Degree of analysis referred to the sort of accounts which tutors gave about what was happening in classrooms. Throughout the transcripts there was evidence of tutors' direct responses to these happenings. It was this sort of data which showed most clearly the spontaneity of their responses to specific situations, e.g.:

> *Tutor 8:* '... the student was doing all kinds of things that you were actually itching to tell her about and to offer advice on and I, when I went in, I sort of barged in too early and wanted to say all these things to the student.... I only got through half the things I badly wanted to say.'

Responses from tutors were very often elicited when things were going wrong:

> *Tutor 8:* 'Yes the inadequacies if you like, in that situation stand out ... they jump out and hit you as you walk in the room.'
>
> *Investigator:* 'Can you say what they are? Summarize some of the things that stand out?

Tutor 8:   'Yes, children doing inappropriate things, children ungainfully occupied . . . well they are so obvious.'

It was noticeable with this tutor that on all the occasions when she was invited to be specific about the problems of this student she quite quickly appealed to the 'obvious' nature of the problems. Tutor 9, on the other hand, was more specific:

Tutor 9:   '. . . but what I saw happening in the classroom for the morning was the most depressing aspect of it all. It was just terrible. It is a first and second year Junior class, half primary 1 as they are called . . . Junior 1, I suppose . . . were doing Maths and Junior 2 were doing Language and Language consisted of the most foul book I have ever seen. They didn't know what they were doing — the quality of the work was just terrible. The quality of the work in the Maths thing which S had arranged for them was some sort of number pattern work — that was dreadful. It entailed drawing lines as arcs on a circle to build up a pattern, like a curved stitching type of thing — but they didn't take any care as to whether they actually lined up their rulers properly — they wobbled their lines, they smudged them, they made such a total mess that most of them couldn't actually see a pattern by the time they had finished. And what distressed me was that S seemed only able to sit on top of it. I never heard her say to any child any remark at all which implied that there was any other way to do it. . . . There were no targets for the children to work towards. No signals at all how they might work, and therefore the whole thing was scrappy.'

In contrast with the account by Tutor 8, this one is a much more specific description of things that were wrong in that classroom. If the first stage is an *intuitive feeling* of all the things that are wrong and the second is a more *detailed description* of specific aspects of the problem, the third is the *search for causes*. This can be illustrated by comparing two accounts:

Tutor 9:   '. . . almost nothing seemed to be working and I suppose the lowest level of what was not working was the management of the children and her interaction with the children . . . . She was asking them to do things and they were complying in a sense that they did things but they weren't the things that she was asking them to do, and what was interesting was that she didn't actually recognize that the children weren't doing what she asked them to do. It was

almost like I know the tune and I know the words —
teachers say right get out your books and in this case it
was write me a poem about ... and they got out their
books and wrote the date and they copied out what she
had written on the board and they went through all the
sort of rituals that kids had learned and it wasn't at all
what she had asked them to do, and I felt that that was
the point at which I had to get in there and talk about
contacting the children.'

Tutor 4: responded to this as follows:

'Mine was a bit like that — a bit more subtle in that S
knows the class is wrong. Some of the time she is picking
up intuitively that the chemistry is not right, the children
are being inattentive, fiddling, disinterested, switched off,
but she is not acting upon what her own intuition is, tells
her to do ... because, I think after discussion we decided
it was because in the earlier days she was anxious to maintain the patterns of working to which the children were
accustomed, that she couldn't, she said, be herself and
relax. Consequently, she never really got a rapport with
the children. She's aware of this cultural gap, she doesn't
know how to bridge it now so she is floundering. We
discussed it at great length and decided that somehow she
had to be more herself. She faced up to it which I think
was good — she saw what the problem was and the upshot
of the discussions were that the target should be that when
a message came through to her that say John was doing
something he shouldn't be doing — that was when the
children were disinterested or whatever, then she acted on
it there and then.'

Here Tutor 9 gave a detailed account of unacceptable happenings in the
classroom, while Tutor 4, recognizing this description, showed the next stage
by describing attempts to examine the underlying reasons. In fact the later
accounts from the student of Tutor 9 showed that she also was aware of
some of the underlying problems in the classroom and later the tutor
responded in the way that Tutor 4 had done.

The purpose here is to illustrate three stages in the accounts of classroom life. These have been called: i) intuitive, ii) descriptive, and iii) analytical. The accounts which tutors gave, the evidence which they used and the
level of analysis which they undertook were different for different tutors,
related to how they dealt with the teaching practice situation.

Confidence. The degree of confidence which tutors attached to the
judgment they made was apparent in some of the accounts. It is quite

difficult to illustrate this because it was often expressed by a spontaneous readiness to respond or by a look of surprise at a query. However, tutors were sometimes asked by their colleagues to express a degree of confidence by being asked 'are you sure?'. Tutor 11, for example, was sure that S1 would not try group work and also that he did not need to allow students to raise issues in discussion since he was able to recognize the most important ones. Similarly, Tutor 8 referred to the problems in S5's classroom as being 'so obvious and yet sadly not to the student who appears to be quite happy with the situation as it is'. The tutor was questioned about this and remained convinced, holding that judgment until the last session when she said, without appearing to notice the discrepancy:

> S5 is a good example of that (i.e. learning what you should do but not how to do it) because she has known what she should do, not only towards the end of this practice but probably towards the middle of the first T.P ... she knew exactly what she should do, so much so that she could have written her own report.'

Other tutors were much more cautious about the judgments they made, often putting forward more than one possibility. In many of the accounts of Tutor 2 there were examples of the use of 'I think' and 'it's possible that' and 'I wonder', all illustrative of her cautious approach to making judgments. This exploratory attitude was also illustrated by the comments of Tutors 4 and 14, whereas Tutors 1 and 5 spoke with considerable confidence. It is important to note that in this sample of tutors, lack of confidence in making judgments tended not to signal uncertainty or lack of conviction but rather a strong element of caution in making absolute judgment about students.

Speed. Tutors were very different in the time it took them to 'weigh things up'. The transcripts often showed the frustration of tutors that they had not made judgments quickly enough. Tutor 9 at the end of the teaching practice bemoaned the fact that she had not recognized the reality of one situation in the early stages:

> *Tutor 9:* 'I think it was a dreadful experience for her because it's only now I realize, through force of circumstances, that she had no model on which to base her action. I thought she had the wherewithall within herself to manage because she had been good in other situations — that she could transfer some of these skills. It turns out that she couldn't and she didn't have anybody to show her the way.'

Very often this speed of judgment, or lack of it, was expressed by tutors at the end of the practice when they felt that by the time they had reached an understanding it was too late:

> *Tutor 3*: '... it's only when you get to the end that you look back and realize that you haven't given some people the right help.'
>
> *Tutor 2*: Well, I suppose that I was a bit tentative at first and trying ... to weigh everything up and thinking how I might contribute well ... but I don't feel in some instances as if I've trusted my own judgment enough.... I feel I should have gone in, I felt I should and yet I didn't because I was frightened to in case I was going to upset a difficult situation.'

The last account in particular shows the close relationship which there can be between speed and confidence. This tutor had made tentative judgments but did not have the confidence in those judgments to act quickly. Tutor 9, however, simply did not have enough information upon which to make a judgment and so found it difficult to make up her mind how to act.

Speed was also related to range. A tutor who worked from a narrow range of possibilities from which to judge could make decisions quickly, although in view of the results not necessarily effectively. Tutors who could appreciate a wide range of possibilities might take longer to chose from these. Tutor 11 was an exception who worked from a wide range but usually made judgments quickly and with confidence.

Implications of the Analysis of Supervision Behaviour for the Development of Reflective Practice

It is hard to imagine that tutors can promote reflective practice in student teachers without being reflective themselves. However, tutors practise supervision in comparative isolation (Rust, 1988) with little opportunity to discuss their practice with colleagues, and supervision has not received the detailed attention which has been given to classroom teaching. The analysis above offers a starting point for thinking about strategies by which tutors might enhance reflective practice.

Sharing the Assessment of the Situation

Making explicit how tutors judge situations and people and take actions, makes it possible for them to share this process with the other people involved, i.e. teachers and student teachers. It has been suggested that judgments about the school environment and the personality characteristics of the participants are important to tutors but these judgments could be shared. Take the example of the tutor who praises all the actions of the student teacher because she/he recognizes a lack of confidence. If the tutor is able to make this motivation explicit, then it is much less likely that the student teacher will get a false impression of the progress of the teaching practice. At the same time, it will be possible to chart, jointly, a sensible professional progression for the student teacher which will probably involve her/him becoming proficient in a limited way and then building on success to develop more ambitious teaching objectives.

Clearly, discussion like that needs to be conducted with sensitivity and this may be even more the case when the nature of the classroom environment is under discussion, for example, whether a student may be innovative in a 'traditional' school environment. However, the evidence from this study suggested that the worries of tutors about opposing the ethos of the school were, often, unjustified providing that shared discussion was made possible. For example, when a tutor felt that the teaching tradition in the school was very formal, it was still possible to encourage group work which was shared by teacher and student teacher in an effective way. In practice, discussion of this type and considerable potential for the development of a reflective approach because it involved people with different beliefs.

Developing Reflective Practice

The point has already been made above that supervision is a lonely occupation, rarely discussed in detail with more than a few colleagues, with a result that tutors are often unaware of their own procedures let alone those of other people. If the outline of tutors' thinking as set out above is close enough to their practice, then there seem to be possibilities for enhancing reflective practice in student teachers.

The analysis suggested that tutors had a common concern with efficacy in particular situations. If this concern could be shared with other tutors it would offer important opportunities for discussion about the nature of teaching competence. Perhaps even more importantly there could be the opportunity for discussion with teacher and student teacher about the nature of efficacy in a particular classroom and the parameters which influenced the judgments being made. It is such discussions which would lead to 'widening the range of criteria which will influence the reflective/critical process' and 'building up a personal set of criteria as a result of the reflective/critical process' which were discussed at the beginning of this paper. The same argument would apply to the sharing of personal views about teaching providing that tutor, teacher and student teacher are able to express those views. The possibilities for developing a high level of 'degree of analysis' look significant and certainly worth exploring.

An important difference between the thinking of individual tutors was the 'range' of teaching behaviour to which they gave their attention. Making these differences explicit offers the possibilities of extending the 'range' of individual tutors' thinking and, subsequently, the range of teaching behaviours which student teachers might consider. Particularly noticeable in the thinking of tutors showing a wide range was their predisposition to find relationships between aspects of teaching and to look for reasons for behaviour which were not readily apparent. This tended to be related to a similar willingness to analyze teaching in a critical, open-minded way, i.e. to go beyond the intuitive understanding of what was taking place to more detailed accounts and to analysis of underlying reasons and motivations. It is these qualities which are characteristic of the reflective approach defined at the beginning of this paper. If the 'range' and 'degree of analysis' in tutors' practice is developed then it seems likely that it will also influence their conceptions of efficacy and reflection about their own personal approaches to teaching.

Drawing on Theoretical Approaches to Supervision

A question still to be addressed is the value or otherwise of theoretical approaches to supervision. Rowell and Dawson (1981) express serious misgivings about the development of professional knowledge which does not, at some time, draw on theoretical insights.

Four main approaches were outlined at the beginning of the chapter:

- a skill-based approach;
- an approach designed to draw on the professional knowledge of the co-operating, classroom teacher;
- a clinical supervision approach;
- a psychopedagogical approach.

A combination of approaches was also seen to be possible.

Some studies of supervision have suggested that tutors are not able to make effective use of theoretical recommendations about supervision. However, in the studies outlined above references were made in the discussion to the theoretical approaches to supervision, and tutors sometimes recognized in these approaches descriptions of what they actually did in classrooms. Just as often they rejected an approach on the grounds that it was not appropriate for a particular situation with a particular student. For example, a clinical approach was seen to be totally appropriate in the case of one student but totally inappropriate in the case of another, who according to the tutor would not raise any professional issue at all if given total control over the professional discussion. Similarly, it was argued that the analytical approach advocated by Stones (1984) would not be helpful for a student who was having serious difficulties since the detailed discursive approach would only lead to greater uncertainty and confusion. For such a student it would be helpful to use a skill-based approach, provided that the skills were those which were directly relevant to those which the class teacher was already using. At the same time, a teacher/student pair working well together in a classroom could be provoked into a justificatory discussion by a planning session exploring certain theoretical principles. What these tutors were showing was the way in which they adapted their approach to meet the needs of the situation as they perceived it. This raises the possibility that if tutors can become more aware of the way they make judgments and the procedures they use as a result of those judgments, they may be able to draw on theoretical models in a meaningful way. To put this another way, tutors may be able to enhance their professional knowledge by becoming more aware of the nature of that knowledge and matching it with theoretical principles. In this way they are likely to enhance the professional experience of the student teachers with whom they are working.

For example, take a student teacher who is judged by the tutor to be lacking in confidence and efficacy in a particular classroom but who is working with a teacher whom the tutor believes to be very competent indeed but expecting too much of the student teacher. The tutor will want to take action to achieve efficacy. This is likely to be at the technical teaching level (Zeichner and Liston, 1987). Teacher and tutor may well use a skill-based approach to supervision in order to achieve efficacy. Reflective thinking will be focused on the most successful practice of certain skills. However, with the achievement of efficacy, the student teacher will be in a position to reflect about the rationale for adopting a particular teaching strategy (Zeichner and Liston 1987). Under these circumstances a different approach to supervision may be appropriate, perhaps a psychopedagogical approach or a clinical approach or a combination of the two. With the increasing competency of the student teacher more general ethical considerations (see Zeichner and Liston (1987), raised through a clinical approach to the supervision, may come to take precedence. In this way the supervision approach will be matched to the classroom situation in a way which is under the control of the participants.

The major difficulty for tutors is the lack of time which they have in classrooms in order to be able to evaluate the situation. As an alternative to proposing systems of supervision, researchers could focus usefully on helping tutors to search out the necessary evidence upon which to make judgments about their actions.

Conclusions

Potentially, tutors who are supervising student teachers in classrooms have the opportunity to influence the reflective practice of those student teachers. However, evidence from studies suggests that the supervision cannot be effective because tutors are not able to do what they intend to do and appear not to be aware of their inadequacies. It has been suggested that this assessment of supervision behaviour does not really do justice to the way tutors work and the careful, if intuitive, judgments which many of them make before they take action in classrooms. Rather than formulate complex supervision strategies and then berate tutors for their inadequacies in implementing them, there is an alternative approach. Working from a model of how tutors actually make judgments, a training programme may be developed which builds on the strengths of that approach and helps tutors to acquire the information they need in order to apply theoretical approaches which will enhance reflective practice.

References

ASHTON, P.M.E., HENDERSON, E.S., MERRIT, J.E. and MORTIMER, D.J. (1983) *Teacher Education in the Classroom: Initial and In-Service*, London and Canberra: Croom Helm.

BROWN, S., MCINTYRE, D. and MCALPINE, A. (1988) *The Knowledge which Underpins the Craft of Teaching*, Edinburgh: Scottish Council for Research in Education.

COGAN, M.L. (1973) *Clinical Supervision*, Boston: Houghton Mifflin.

ELBAZ, F. (1990) 'Knowledge and Discourse: Evolution of Research on Teacher Thinking', in DAY, C., POPE, M. and DENICOLO, P. (eds) *Insight into Teacher Thinking and Practice*, London: The Falmer Press.

GITLIN, A., ROSE, E., WALTHER, C. and MAGLEBY, L. (1985) 'Why Supervisors Behave as They Do: Relationship of beliefs, Socialisation and Practice', *Journal of Education for Teaching*, **11**(1), pp. 50–62.

GOLDHAMMER, R. (1969) *Clinical Supervision*, New York: Holt, Rinehart and Winston.

GRANT, C.A. and ZEICHNER, K. (1984) 'On Becoming a Reflective Teacher', in GRANT, C.A. (ed.) *Preparing for Reflective Teaching*, Boston: Allyn Bacon.

GRIFFITHS, R. (1974) 'The Training of Micro-Teaching Supervisors', *British Journal of Teacher Education*, **1**(2), pp. 59–78.

HARGREAVES, D.H., HESTOR, S.K. and MELLOR, F.J. (1975) *Deviance in Classrooms*, London and Boston: Routledge and Kegan Paul.

HEATH, R.W. and NEILSON, M.A. (1974) 'Performance Based Teacher Education', *Review of Educational Research*, **44**, pp. 463–84.

LOWYCK, J. (1986) 'Post-Interactive Reflections of Teachers: a Critical Appraisal', in BEN-PERTZ, M., BROMME, R. and HALKES, R. (eds) *Advances in Research on Teacher Thinking*, Lisse: Swets and Zeitlinger.

MCALPINE, A., BROWN, S., MCINTYRE, D. and HAGGER, H. (1988) *Student Teachers learning from Experienced Teachers*, Scottish Council for Research in Teacher Education Project Report, Edinburgh: Scottish Council for Research in Education.

MCNAMARA, D.R. and DESFORGES, C. (1978) 'The Social Sciences, Teacher Education and Objectification of Craft Knowledge', *British Journal of Teacher Education*, **4**(1), pp. 17–36.

MANSFIELD, P.A. (1986) 'Patchwork Pedagogy: A Case Study of Supervisors' Emphasis on Pedagogy in Post-Lesson Conference', *Journal of Education for Teaching*, **12**(3), pp. 259–71.

ROWELL, J.A. and DAWSON, C.J. (1981) 'Prepared to Teach?', *Journal of Education for Teaching*, **7**(3), pp. 315–323.

RUST, F.O. (1988) 'How Supervisors Think about Teaching', *Journal of Teacher Education*, **39**(2), pp. 56–63.

SHANKER, A. (1974) *Competency-Based Teacher Training and Certification: Acceptable and Unacceptable Models*, Washington, D.C.: Quest Books.

SHAVELSON, R.J. and STERN, P. (1981) 'Research on Teachers' Pedagogical Thoughts, Judgments, Decisions and Behaviour', *Review of Educational Research*, **51**, pp. 455–98.

SOLOMAN, J. (1987) 'New Thoughts of Teacher Education', *Oxford Review of Education*, **13**(3), pp. 267–74.

STONES, E. (1984) *Supervision in Teacher Education*, London: Methuen.

TERRELL, C., TREGASKIS, O., BOYDELL, D. (1985) *Teaching Practice Supervisors in Primary Schools: an Ethnomethodological Perspective*, a research report of Cheltenham College of St Paul and St Mary.

TURNEY, C., CAIRNS, L.G., ELTIS, K.J., HATTON, N., THEW, D.M., TOWLER, J. and WRIGHT, R. (1982) *The Practicum in Teacher Education: Research, Practice and Supervision*, Sydney: Sydney University Press.

ZEICHNER, N. and LISTON, D. (1987) 'Teaching Student Teachers to Reflect', *Harvard Educational Review*, **57**(1), pp. 23–47.

ZEICHNER, K. and TABACHNICK, B.R. (1982) 'The Belief Systems of University Supervisors in an Elementary Student Teaching Programme', *Journal of Education for Teaching*, **8**(1), pp. 34–54.

7 Changes in Beliefs About Learners Among Participants in Eleven Teacher Education Programs

G. Williamson McDiarmid

Virtually all treatments of teacher knowledge address the issue of teachers' knowledge and beliefs about learners (see, for example, Hawkins, 1974; Kerr, 1981; Schwab, 1960/1978). The knowledge and beliefs about learners that teachers need is, of course, a matter of debate. Although educators, policymakers, and others may disagree on issues such as what teachers need to know about the culture of the home and community from which children come, they do seem to agree on some broad themes. The first of these is that teachers need to look beyond students' external attributes — their race, ethnicity, gender, language or dialect, social class and disabilities — and focus instead on students' potential as learners. Another commonality seems to be that teachers' responsibilities include working hard with all children, regardless of their past achievement and apparent capacity to understand a given subject, to insure that they learn. This means exerting at least as much effort with those who, for whatever reason, are having a hard time getting it as with those who seem to have a proclivity for a particular idea or procedure. An associated idea is that teachers need to expect and communicate to students their expectation that all children can learn, whatever is included in the school curriculum.

The importance of these ideas in the eyes of educators and policymakers is manifest in the ubiquity in the U.S. of the required course in psychology as a part of preservice teacher education programs. Other learning opportunities for prospective and practising teachers, such as courses or workshops in multicultural education and in the social foundations of education, focus on these same themes. A primary purpose of such opportunities is to convince prospective teachers, if they need convincing, of the moral and evidential bases of the three points above — namely, that all children are innately capable of learning and teachers are morally and legally obliged to teach all children; that race, ethnicity, gender and social class are unrelated to children's capacities to learn; and that teachers hold and communicate their expectations for learning to their students.

What effect do such opportunities have on teachers' beliefs about learners? Do they, in fact, after teacher education programs, believe all students are capable of learning whatever is part of the school curriculum? What role do they believe attributes such as sex or ethnicity should play in teachers' instructional decision-making? Do they believe they should expect the same of all students, that all students should be held to the same standards? These are some of the questions on which researchers at the National Center for Research on Teacher Education collected data as part of the Teacher Education and Learning to Teach (TELT) study. A four-year longitudinal investigation of the developing knowledge of teachers enrolled in eleven preservice, induction, alternate route and inservice programs, TELT was conducted between 1987 and 1990 (Kennedy, Ball, McDiarmid and Schmidt, in press; McDiarmid and Ball, 1989).

Methodology

The Sample of Programs

Teacher education programs in the TELT sample were selected to represent variations in structure, settings, conceptual orientation, and the types of programs — that is, preservice, inservice, induction and alternate route (Table 7.1; for more on the sample, see Kennedy, Ball, McDiarmid and Schmidt, in press). Although structurally conventional undergraduate programs that include two years of liberal arts and two years of professional studies predominate in the sample, we also included a five-year program, summer staff development programs that incorporated classroom support, and a master's program that enlists veteran teachers to support first-year teachers.

We also tried to represent variation in the institutional settings for teacher education. Hence, the sample includes university-based preservice programs, including one at an historically black institution, staff development programs that had a foot in universities but also a foot in the schools, one alternate route program organized and run by an urban school district and another operated by a state department of education, and an induction program for first-year teachers jointly run by a university and an urban school district.

By conceptual orientation we mean both the view of the nature of the knowledge teachers need in order to teach (scientific, liberal, or skill/craft) and the view of the pedagogy in the program (generic or subject-specific). For instance, among the preservice programs, we included a program that purported to base its curriculum and view of teaching on research on teaching (scientific), defined in this case as process-product research. Another preservice program claimed to focus on prospective teachers' understanding of the subjects they would be teaching (subject-specific conception of pedagogy) and the kinds of problems learners typically encounter in learning about these subjects. A third preservice program in the sample evolved from the normal school-teachers college tradition and offered a conventional curriculum (generic conception of pedagogy), reflecting the tradition from which it developed — a sequence of educational psychology, social and philosophical foundations, methods, reading methods and student teaching. Yet a fourth program professed to focus on the community and families but, in fact, was overtaken during our study by the need to prepare prospective teachers for state-mandated tests required for certification. Finally, the fifth preservice program housed in a prestigious liberal arts college was designed to capitalize on the academic strengths of students' backgrounds and their liberal arts studies and to shape their moral and social commitments.

The Sample of Teachers

We collected data from all participants in each of the programs we studied. At a minimum, we collected baseline questionnaire data on virtually all participants we could contact, a total of nearly 700. For each program, we randomly selected a small intensive subsample. Because we wanted to collect considerable data on these individuals at three and, in some cases, four points in time over a two- to three-year period, we limited the intensive subsample to between twelve and sixteen participants from each program. In one case, the total number of participants was so small we included all of them in the intensive subsample.

Attrition from the questionnaire sample for the preservice and alternate route samples was high — more than 50 per cent. Some 257 students in the original preservice sample of 405 did not complete questionnaires at the end of their programs. Tracking down seniors during their last term in school and convincing them to complete a 309-item questionnaire proved most difficult. Normally, such an attrition rate would fatally flaw a study. However, our retention rate for participants in the *intensive* sample was high — above 90 per cent for the sample. The intensive sample was selected to represent all participants in each program. Consequently, we can view those who completed the questionnaires at the end of their programs to be reasonably representative of all participants in the program. We did not, however, follow up on those respondents who dropped out of the study.

Data Collection

We used three instruments to track changes in teachers' knowledge, skills and dispositions: a conventional questionnaire, an interview consisting

Table 7.1 Description of the Teacher Education Programs included in the TELT Sample

Program	Conception of Knowledge for Teaching	Conception of Pedagogy	Structure	Setting
Preservice				
PROTEACH, Univ. of Florida	Scientific	Generic	Elem: 5 year Sec: BA + 5th yr.	Large state research university
Academic Learning, Michigan State Univ.	Not clear	Subject-specific	4 years; mentors; 3-course math sequence	Large state research university
Teacher Education, Dartmouth College	Liberal	Generic	4 years	Small, elite liberal arts college
Teacher Education, Illinois State Univ.	Not clear	Generic	4 years; methods blocks	Large state university (former teachers' college)
Teacher Education, Norfolk State Univ.	Scientific	Generic	4 years	Historically black, urban institution

Table 7.1 continued

Program	Conception of Knowledge for Teaching	Conception of Pedagogy	Structure	Setting
Alternate Route				
Provisional Teacher Program, New Jersey	Skill/Craft	Generic	Summer classes; weekend sessions	State department of education
Teacher Training Program, LAUSD	Skill/Craft	Generic	Summer; mentors; multicultural week	Large urban school district
Induction				
Graduate Intern/Teacher Induction, U NM-Albuquerque Schools	Not clear	Generic	Classes for MA; visits from and seminars with clinical teachers	Urban school district-state university collaboration
Staff Development				
SummerMath, Mt Holyoke	Not clear	Subject-specific	Summer institute; classroom follow-up	Summer program at a liberal arts college
Teachers College Writing Project	Skill/Craft	Subject-specific	Summer institute; support in classrooms	Urban university-school district cooperation

largely of classroom scenarios, and an observation guide (Kennedy *et al.*, in press). We developed the instruments as a package in an attempt to compensate for the weaknesses in each. The questionnaire consisted of some 309 items, most of them seven-point Likert-scale statements or forced-choice items, designed to tap teachers' beliefs about and knowlege of: the teaching and learning of mathematics and writing; the teacher's role in the teaching and learning of mathematics and writing; mathematics typically taught in school; conventions of written standard English; learners; and teachers as learners, writers and knowers of mathematics.

Some forty-five items on the questionnaire were intended to tap teachers' views of learners. Just as teachers' beliefs tend to reinforce one another and together constitute 'webs', the items did not unambiguously elicit teachers' beliefs about learners only. Teachers' beliefs about mathematics and writing — what these subjects are, what it means to know and learn them, how these subjects are best taught — were shaped by and contributed to their beliefs about learners.

Participants in the preservice intensive sample completed the questionnaire and were interviewed at least three times — at the beginning and the end of their programs and during the Spring term of their first year of teaching. (We also observed them student teach and teach in their own classrooms but did not draw on these data for this analysis). Teachers in the inservice, induction and alternative route intensive samples also completed the questionnaires and were interviewed at least three times (and observed in their classrooms at least once).

Analysis

The analysis and discussion below focuses on ten of the questionnaire items designed to tap teachers' beliefs about learners. In addition, on the interview, most questions required teachers to discuss, directly or indirectly, their views of learners. Questions about learners were often questions about differences among learners. Given the trend towards classrooms that are increasingly diverse — socially, ethnically, culturally — questions about differences are of immediate moment to teacher educators. Consequently, we explore below teachers' responses to one of the scenarios to which teachers were asked to respond on the interview. This scenario describes a classroom situation involving students from different ethnic backgrounds.

We analyzed questionnaire and interview data collected at the beginning and at the end of the programs. For those participants from whom we had both beginning-of-program and end-of-program data, we computed simple frequencies for each item by program type — i.e. preservice, induction, alternate route and inservice. In addition, we conducted two-tail t-tests on these data to determine the significance of beginning-of-program to end-of-program differences. Using the two-tail t-test insures that only those cases for which we have valid responses to a given item for both points in time will be included.

Limitations

The small size and purposive nature of our sample of programs limited the generalizability of our findings. At the same time, the programs in our sample were chosen to represent common variations in teacher education. The sample enabled us to explore critical issues and questions in teacher knowledge, beliefs and learning in the context of representative programs.

We also relied heavily on self-reported data collected with question-naires and interviews. Talking about teaching and doing it are not the same. We were interested principally, however, in teachers' knowledge and beliefs and how these change over time, phenomena that are difficult to observe and measure given the way we defined these (McDiarmid and Ball, 1989).

Beliefs about the Role of Gender in Mathematical and Writing Ability

We couched our questions about students' capacities to learn in the context of specific subject matters — namely, mathematics and writing. These subject matters provided the teachers' contexts for responding to questions as well as the researchers' contexts for interpreting the teachers' responses. Teachers' dispositions to take responsibility for ensuring that all children have the opportunity to learn the academic content available in schools is, logically, linked to their beliefs about academic ability and the degree to which ability is innate and the degree to which it is malleable. Teachers who believe, for instance, that 'to be good at math, you need to have a kind of "mathematical mind"', or that some students can 'simply never be good at writing' may be more inclined to give up earlier on students who seem to have difficulties in mathematics or learning to write. Why not focus on something for which the student appears to have an aptitude? Beliefs about students' capacities to learn mathematics is particularly critical because, historically, girls and children of colour have achieved below the level of white boys and have been less likely to pursue more advanced mathematics (National Research Council, 1989). On the other hand, teachers who believe that ability in mathematics and writing is largely innate may also view the lack of 'innate' ability as a challenge to which they should rise rather than a reason to stop trying.

As Figure 7.1 reveals, *preservice* teachers in the TELT sample tend to disagree with the idea that girls are naturally better at writing than are boys at the outset of their programs. By the end of their program, they are even

Figure 7.1: Means of Teachers' Responses at the Beginning and End of Preservice, Induction, Alternate Route and Inservice Programs to the Statement: **'In general, girls tend to be naturally better than boys at writing.'**

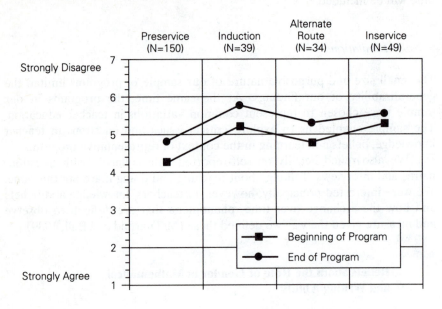

Significance of Change

Preservice	Induction	Alternate Route	Inservice
p < .001	p < .05	n.s.	n.s.

more likely to disagree. Although the change in the mean appears small, it is none the less statistically significant.

Induction teachers were, at the beginning of the programs, even more likely to disagree with the idea of a natural edge for girls in writing than were their preservice counterparts. By the end of their program — in this case, after their first year of teaching — they were even more likely to disagree and the difference is statistically significant.

The responses of teachers in the *alternate route* programs reveal the same pattern. They disagreed with the statement at the beginning of the program and the level of disagreement grew over time. The difference in their case is not, however, significant. Finally, few *inservice* teachers, either at the beginning or end of their programs, agreed with the idea that girls are naturally better in writing. The difference between the beginning and end was slight and not statistically significant.

Figure 7.2 reveals similar patterns for teachers' responses to the statement that 'boys tend to be naturally better at math than girls'. Most teachers

Figure 7.2: *Means of Teachers' Responses at the Beginning and End of Preservice, Induction, Alternate Route and Inservice Programs to the Statement:* **'In general, boys tend to be naturally better at math than girls.'**

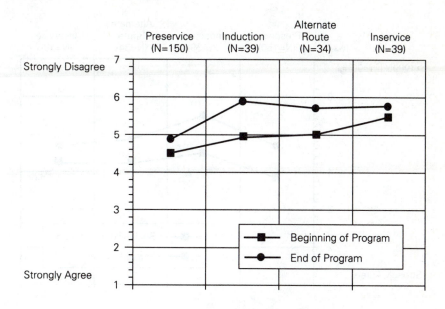

Significance of Change

Preservice	Induction	Alternate Route	Inservice
p < .05	p < .000	p < .05	n.s.

in all four types of program disagreed with the statement at the beginning of their programs and the level of disagreement increased by the end of the programs. In three of the four types of program, the difference between the beginning and end of the program was statistically significant. A change of nearly a full point on the seven-point Likert scale distinguishes the change on the responses of the induction teachers at the beginning and end of their program. Not only does this represent the largest beginning-to-end difference on this item but it is one of the greatest changes measured on any of the learner items presented here.

In sum, few teachers in any of the four types of programs — preservice, induction, alternate route, and inservice — appeared to believe, at the outset of their programs, that ability in either writing or mathematics is related to gender. Not represented in the tables of means are the sizeable proportions of teachers who indicated that they were unsure about this issue. By the end of their programs, most teachers in the TELT sample appeared more

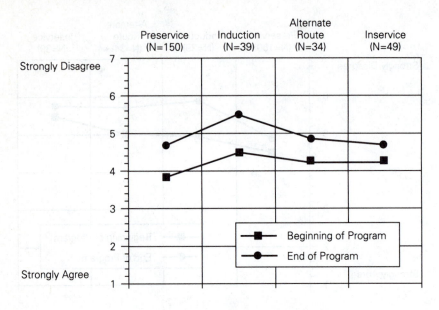

Figure 7.3: Means of Teachers' Responses at the Beginning and End of Preservice, Induction, Alternate Route and Inservice Programs to the Statement: 'To be good at mathematics, you need to have a kind of "mathematical mind".'

Significance of Change

Preservice	Induction	Alternate Route	Inservice
p < .000	p < .000	p = .05	n.s.

convinced that neither sex has a 'natural' advantage over the other in either writing or mathematics.

Teachers Beliefs about Whether Abilities in Mathematics and Writing are Innate

We constructed several other items to gauge teachers' beliefs in the innateness of academic ability. As Figure 7.3 shows, *preservice teachers*, at the outset, tended, by a slight margin, to agree that 'to be good in mathematics, you need to have a kind of "mathematical mind".' By the end of their programs, however, fewer preservice teachers agreed with the statement, a statistically significant difference. Teachers in the *induction sample* tended to disagree, at the beginning of their program, with the idea that a 'mathematical mind' is necessary to be good at mathematics. By the end of their program, even fewer agreed with this notion — again, a difference that is statistically significant.

Fewer *alternate route teachers* at the end than at the beginning of the programs seemed to believe in the notion of 'mathematical mind'. The pattern among *inservice* teachers was similar, although the beginning-to-end difference was not statistically significant.

We also asked teachers about ability in writing. We asked them to respond to the statement that 'to be good at writing, you need to produce polished prose with ease'. This statement makes effortless production of text the primary criterion for success, a view at odds with both how professional writers work and current thinking in the field of composition that holds that being good at writing often entails iterative revisions as an author strives to work out his/her ideas in a voice that communicates to a particular audience. Consequently, a good writer is not necessarily one who produces 'polished prose' easily but rather one who revises and reworks his/her text until it fulfils his/her purpose: to communicate particular ideas, beliefs, and feelings to particular audiences.

Teachers who agree with this statement may regard students who struggle to express themselves, who must continually revise and rework their writing, as inferior to those who generate text with facility. Furthermore, they may not be inclined to provide students with opportunities to revise their written work. The issue gains greater significance if the teacher works with children for whom standard English is not their primary language or dialect. Producing 'polished prose', which implies standard English, can be a real struggle for these students as they strive to master a new language.

Teachers in all the programs demonstrated statistically significant changes on this statement (Figure 7.4). Most teachers in the sample began their programs disagreeing with the statement and they came to disagree more decisively over time. The most dramatic differences appeared in programs that emphasized a process approach to the teaching of writing. Yet, the proportion of teachers disagreeing with this statement also increased in those programs that did not have a process writing emphasis. Consequently, these apparent differences in teachers' beliefs between the beginning and end of the various programs may have less to do with beliefs about students in relation to the particular subject matter than with beliefs about students' capacities in general.

On other items designed to elicit teachers' beliefs about learners, we found fewer beginning-to-end differences. For instance, most teachers in all four types of programs disagreed with the statement that 'there are some students who can simply never be any good at writing' at the beginning of their programs and their views did not change significantly (Figure 7.5). In some types of programs — particularly, alternate routes — however, a sizeable minority of those in the sample agreed with the statement.

Large majorities of teachers in all four types of programs agreed with the statement that 'some people are naturally able to organize their thoughts for writing' (Figure 7.6). This view does not appear to have changed significantly from the beginning to the end of the programs.

Figure 7.4: Means of Teachers' Responses at the Beginning and End of Preservice, Induction, Alternate Route and Inservice Programs to the Statement: **'To be good at writing, you need to produce polished prose with ease'.**

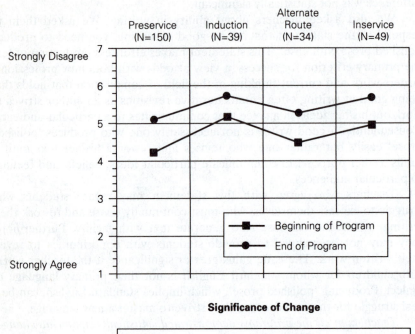

The story these data have to tell of teachers' beliefs about the innateness of ability in mathematics and writing is ambiguous. Most teachers in the sample began their programs believing that a 'mathematical mind' is not a requisite for being good at mathematics nor is facility in producing polished prose a sign of being good at writing. By the end of their programs, teachers' convictions seem to have strengthened. At the same time, considerable majorities believed that some people are 'naturally able to organize their thoughts for writing' and sizeable proportions thought that some students will never be any good at writing. Consequently, while some evidence points to teachers' modifying their beliefs about the innate capacities of students in mathematics and writing, the data also suggest that many teachers in the sample do believe that abilities, particularly in writing, are innate and not easily enhanced. The picture that emerges is more conflicted and complicated than we are led to believe by the soothing sentiments of the 'all-children-can-learn' mantra.

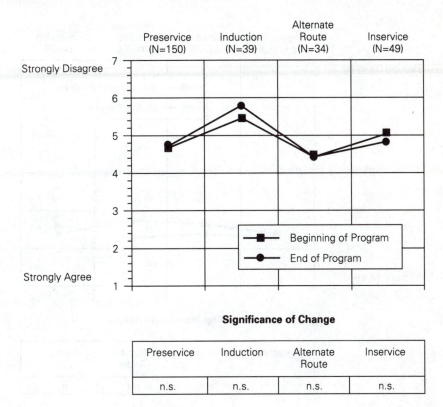

Figure 7.5: *Means of Teachers' Responses at the Beginning and End of Preservice, Induction, Alternate Route and Inservice Programs to the Statement:* **'There are some students who simply can never be any good at writing'.**

Significance of Change

Preservice	Induction	Alternate Route	Inservice
n.s.	n.s.	n.s.	n.s.

Teachers' Beliefs about their own Capacities in Mathematics

Figure 7.7 shows teachers' responses to a related item: 'I don't have the kind of mind needed to do advanced mathematics.' The items about mathematical ability described above asked about ability in others. We intended this item to gauge how teachers thought about their own ability in mathematics as opposed to how they thought about ability in others. Notice, in Figure 7.7, that teachers in the *preservice* and *induction* programs appear to become less convinced that they don't have the right kind of mind for mathematics. As noted above, significant proportions of teachers in these two programs also seemed to change their views about whether mathematical ability is innate and related to gender. A number of *alternate route teachers* also appear to have reconsidered their own capacity to do advanced math but the difference is not quite statistically significant. Most of the *inservice teachers*

Figure 7.6: *Means of Teachers' Responses at the Beginning and End of Preservice, Induction, Alternate Route and Inservice Programs to the Statement:* **'Some people are naturally better able to organize their thoughts for writing'.**

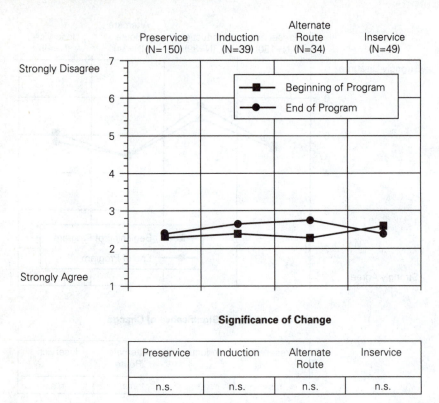

Significance of Change

Preservice	Induction	Alternate Route	Inservice
n.s.	n.s.	n.s.	n.s.

disagreed with the statement at the beginning of their programs and didn't appear to change significantly.

Figure 7.7 and the others discussed above suggest that, at least on the issue of their own mathematical ability and that of others, some teachers — specifically those in preservice and induction programs — did appear to change their views somewhat during their involvement with formal teacher education programs. A number of alternate route teachers also seemed to change their beliefs although the difference is not statistically significant. More experienced teachers appeared to hold beliefs about learners and themselves towards which many of the less experienced teachers seem to be moving. The direction of change is toward believing that the capacity to learn mathematics is not fixed but rather is amenable to instruction, that boys may not have a natural edge in learning mathematics, and that the teachers themselves may be capable of learning advanced mathematics. Of particular significance is the relationship, suggested but by no means proved by the data, between teachers' beliefs about themselves as learners of

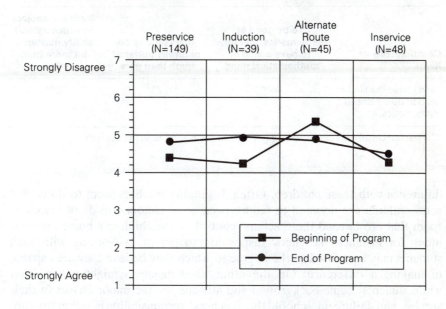

Figure 7.7: Means of Teachers' Responses at the Beginning and End of Preservice, Induction, Alternate Route and Inservice Programs to the Statement: **'I can handle basic mathematics, but I don't have the kind of mind needed to do advanced mathematics'.**

Significance of Change

Preservice	Induction	Alternate Route	Inservice
p < .01	p < .05	p < .05	n.s.

mathematics and their beliefs about others as learners of mathematics. Although the data do not allow us to determine causation, what may be important is that teachers' views of students' capacities and capabilities may be related to their perceptions of their own capacities and capabilities.

To find out if, as we supposed, teachers' beliefs about the extent to which mathematical ability is fixed in others are associated with their beliefs about their own capacity to do advanced mathematics, we correlated these items. As Table 7.2 reveals, all the coefficients for these items were positive and statistically significant (at the p > .01 level) suggesting that, indeed, these beliefs may be related.

Teachers' Beliefs about the Source of Children's Success in School

Given the relatively high rates of school failure of poor children and those of colour, a critical issue is whether or not teachers believe they can make a

Table 7.2   Correlation of Preservice, Induction, Alternate Route and Inservice Teachers' Views of Mathematical Ability in Others with Their Views of Their Own Ability at the End of Their Teacher Education Programs (N = 284)

Questionnaire Items	To be good at mathematics, you need to have a kind of 'mathematical mind.'	Boys tend to be naturally better at math than girls.	Math is a subject in which natural ability matters a lot more than effort.
I don't have the kind of mind to do advanced mathematics.	.44**	.22**	.18**

** Pearson correlation coefficients significant at the p > .01 level (two-tailed).

difference with these children. Often, beginning teachers seem to think that some children are doomed to failure because of factors outside of the classroom that are beyond the teachers' control — the children's home environment, for instance. Teachers' disposition to persist in working with such students may be related to the degree to which they believe they are capable of making a difference. On the other hand, teachers might believe that while students' home background and attitude are the major factors in their success and failure in school, the teachers' responsibility is either to capitalize upon or overcome these factors.

In current rhetoric — particularly the mantra that 'all children can learn' — teachers are exhorted not to blame children for their failures and to treat all children as capable of learning, whatever is in the school curriculum. Regardless of what they really believe, prospective teachers soon learn to repeat the mantra. Our data reveal, however, that most teachers in our preservice sample — indeed, across all four types of programs in our sample — believed, both at the beginning and the end of their programs, that students themselves primarily determine whether or not they succeed in school, not the teacher.

Less than half of the *preservice teachers* in our sample, both at the beginning and the end of their programs, identified a teacher factor rather than a student factor as the 'most frequent sources' of students' school success (Figure 7.8). Teacher factors included teacher's attention to the unique interests and abilities of students, teacher's use of effective methods, and teacher's enthusiasm or perseverance. Student factors included student's home background, student's intellectual ability, and student's enthusiasm or perseverance. The latter proved to be the most frequently cited source of success across program types.

Nearly half of the *teachers in the induction program* — all of whom were, by definition, first-year teachers — believed, when they started their program, that a teacher factor was the 'almost frequent source' of student school success. Less than 40 per cent believed this at the end — in other

Figure 7.8: *Percentage of Teachers Who Identified a Teacher Factor* (rather than a Student Factor**) as the **Primary Source of Student School Success** at the Beginning and End of Preservice, Induction, Alternate Route and Inservice Programs*

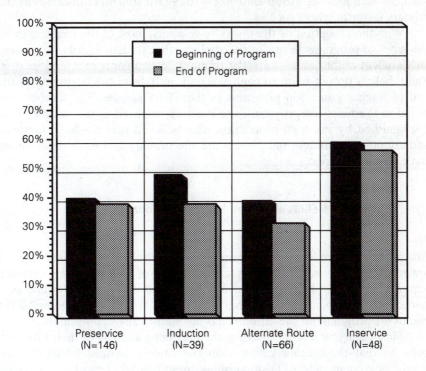

Significance of Change

Preservice	Induction	Alternate Route	Inservice
n.s.	n.s.	n.s	n.s.

* Teacher factors included: teacher's attention to the unique interests and abilities of students, teacher's use of effective methods, and teacher's enthusiasm or perseverance.
** Student factors included: student's home background, student's intellectual ability, and student's enthusiasm or perseverance.

words, after a year in the classroom, although this difference is not statistically significant.

Roughly 40 per cent of the teachers in the *alternate route* programs believed, at the outset, that teacher factors were the 'most frequent source' of school success; even fewer cited a teacher factor after a year of teaching. The difference is not, however, statistically significant. A higher proportion of *inservice teachers* than any other group indicated that they thought the teacher plays the primary role in student success. Fifty-nine per cent at the beginning and 56 per cent at the end chose teacher factors — mainly teaching methods — as the primary source of student success. These experienced teachers were also the group least likely to regard student enthusiasm as the primary factor in school success.

With the exception of the inservice teachers, most of the teachers in all the types of programs in our sample believe that student factors — particularly student enthusiasm — are the primary determinants of school success. These beliefs do not seem to change significantly from the beginning to the end of teacher education programs in the TELT sample. The teachers enrolled in the inservice programs, the most experienced in the sample, were distinguished by the high proportion who believed that teachers' methods and attention to student uniqueness are the primary factors in determining student school success.

Teacher's Beliefs about the Source of Children's Failures in Schools

Just as they believe learners are primarily responsible for their success, most *preservice teachers*, both at the beginning and end of their programs, believed learners are primarily responsible for their failures (Figure 7.9). The proportion of those who chose teacher factors rose from the beginning to the end of the program but the difference is not statistically significant.

Most *induction teachers*, both at the beginning and end of their program, believed that the teacher rather than the student is most frequently the source of student failure. Distinguishing these teachers from those in other types of programs was the belief shared by almost half of them that the teacher's failure to consider student uniqueness was most frequently the source of student failure. Many teachers in this program taught in classrooms that included both Mexican-American and native American children, a circumstance that may have influenced their beliefs.

Most *alternate route teachers* began their programs believing that student factors rather than teacher factors are most frequently responsible for student failure. By the end of the program — that is, at the end of their first year of teaching — significantly more of the teachers in these programs believed this to be true, many citing, in particular, student home background as the source of student failure. Like their counterparts in the alternate route programs, a significant number of teachers in the *inservice programs* also appeared to have changed their beliefs about the source of student failure. The direction of the change, however, was the opposite of that exhibited by many alternate route teachers; whereas most chose student factors as the primary source of failure at the beginning of their programs, only half did so at the end of the program, a statistically significant difference.

In sum, most teachers in the preservice and alternate route programs in the TELT sample began their programs believing that student factors —

Figure 7.9: Percentage of Teachers Who Identified a Teacher Factor* (rather than a Student Factor**) as the **Primary Source of Student School Failure** *at the Beginning and End of Preservice, Induction, Alternate Route and Inservice Programs*

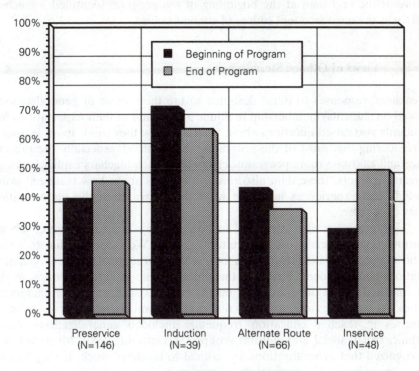

Significance of Change

Preservice	Induction	Alternate Route	Inservice
n.s.	n.s.	p < .05	p < .01

* Teacher factors included: teacher's attention to the unique interests and abilities of students, teacher's use of effective methods, and teacher's enthusiasm or perseverance.
** Student factors included: student's home background, student's intellectual ability, and student's enthusiasm or perseverance.

home background, ability or enthusiasm — not teacher factors — attending to uniqueness, methods, or enthusiasm — are most frequently the source of both students' success and failure in school. Teachers in the induction and inservice programs showed different patterns. Although they seemed to agree with the preservice and alternate route teachers that student factors are most frequently the source of success, most of the induction and inservice teachers attributed students' school failure to teachers, particularly to teachers' failure to consider student uniqueness. Inservice teachers differed from teachers in the other types of programs in that most thought teacher factors were most frequently the source of student success while significantly more at the end than at the beginning of the program identified a teacher factor as the most frequent source of student failure.

Views of Others: Stereotypes

Teachers' responses to items designed to tap their views of generalizations based on students' membership in ethnic groups and of their expectations for students also raised questions about what and how they think about learners. Considering that most of the programs we examined, especially the preservice and alternate route programs, claimed to teach teachers explicitly about diverse learners, these data also raised questions about how teachers' prior beliefs and experiences influence what they learn from the opportunities they encounter.

We are especially interested in how teachers treat information about various ethnic, racial, social or cultural groups. We reasoned that teachers who accepted, as valid information for making instructional decisions, generalizations about students based on their membership in various groups, might be inclined to prejudge students on the basis of such ascriptive characteristics. At the same time, we knew that multicultural courses or cross-cultural courses in teacher education frequently included generalizations about ethnic, racial, social and cultural groups (McDiarmid, 1990). Moreover, we recognized that generalizations are critical to teachers' work. If they had to treat every learner as completely unique, as having nothing in common with other, say, seven-year-olds or adolescent boys, teaching groups of twenty-five or thirty students might be an even more daunting task than it already is. Consequently, we were interested in the two different messages teachers would likely encounter: that generalizations about groups of people are inherently unfair and prejudicial and that generalized information about different groups in society is vital to teaching children from these groups.

On the interview, we presented teachers with a scenario in which they were asked to respond to advice from colleagues about a group of students — specifically native Americans:

> Imagine that you have been hired midway through the school year to take over for a teacher who is going on maternity leave. During the first day, you notice a group of native Americans sitting together at the back of the class, while white and Asian-American students are sitting in front. The native American students don't volunteer to answer questions or to participate in discussions. Later, when you mention this to colleagues in the teachers' lounge, they tell you that the native American students are naturally shy and that asking them questions embarrasses them so it's best not to call on them.

What do you think of the teachers' explanation of the native American students' behavior? How would you deal with the native American students in this class?

In analyzing responses, we coded teachers' reactions to the suggestion that the native American students sat and behaved as they did because of a behavioural characteristic purported to derive from their membership of a particular ethnic group. If in their response the teacher agreed with or did not question the validity of the stereotype. 'Native American students are naturally shy', we coded their response as 'accepts stereotype' (table 12). An example of such a response is:

It could be accurate. . . . My exposure to native American students isn't that great so I don't have many personal experiences to draw upon. That could be a correct . . . generalization. (Alternate route teacher, post-program interview).

In this example, the teacher seems to have no quarrel with using stereotypes of students based on their group membership as an explanation for their behaviour and as a basis for making instructional decisions. Her hesitation comes from not having experienced native American students and, therefore, being somewhat unsure about this particular generalization.

If the teacher seemed unsure about whether or not the generalization was an adequate explanation for the students' behaviour, we coded the response 'unsure':

Well, I mean it could be true but I am not really sure. I think there might be another reason why they wouldn't want to answer questions. (Preservice teacher, post-program interview).

If the teacher rejects the idea that stereotypes based on group membership are a valid basis for explaining students' behaviors or for making instructional decisions, we coded the response as 'rejects stereotype':

It's a generalization. Over generalizing, tagging people. It's prejudice. I think it's completely wrong. (Preservice teacher, post-program interview).

But just to run off a whole group of people and say that whole group, nationality, minority, whatever, is . . . just naturally shy and write it off [and decide] that they don't have to participate — that's silliness. (Alternate route teacher, post-program interview).

Finally, some responses were simply not clear enough to code. In these, the teachers sometimes started with one position but, in explaining their

Table 7.3   Reaction to Scenario Portraying Use of Stereotype as Basis for Making Teaching Decision

Reaction to use of stereotype for native American students	Alternate Route Program		State-Organized Program		Preservice Programs
Data Collection Point	Pre-Workshop	Post-Workshop	Pre-Training	Pre-Training	Post-Program
N=	12	11	17	13	66
Accepts stereotype	33	27	16	23	24
Unsure if stereotype is accurate	17	18	6	8	17
Rejects stereotype	42	45	78	54	36
Not clear if accepts or rejects	8	9	0	15	23
Total*	100%	99%	100%	100%	100%

* Totals less or more than 100% due to rounding.

response, worked their way around to another. Others would seem to reject the stereotype but proceed to respond as if they accepted it as valid.

Table 7.3 presents the responses of teachers enrolled in one of the alternate routes and in all the preservice programs in the TELT sample as well as those involved in a special workshop sponsored by a state department of education that was not part of the TELT sample. The special workshop was an experimental three-day course organized to prepare student teachers for multicultural classrooms (McDiarmid and Price, 1990). The alternate route, organized by a large urban school district, placed particular emphasis on preparing beginning teachers for the culturally, socially, racially and linguistically diverse classrooms typical in the district. Teachers in this program spent a week after their first year of teaching attending workshops on issues in multicultural education (McDiarmid, 1990). We collected extensive data on the presentations and activities teachers experienced in both the state-sponsored and the alternate route multicultural workshops.

Responses of teachers in the two programs — the alternate route and the state-organized — for which we collected data both at the beginning and end of the program reveal little evidence of change. The responses of preservice teachers collected at the end of their programs (unfortunately, we do not have baseline data for these teachers as we developed the scenarios after the first wave of data collection) were not significantly different from those of teachers in the alternate route and state-organized programs.

Moreover, only in the state-organized program did more teachers reject the stereotype than accepted it or were unsure about its validity.

Consequently, between roughly a third and a half of the preservice and alternate route teachers in the TELT sample and student teachers in a state-organized multicultural program seemed inclined to accept stereotypes of native American students as a basis for making instructional decisions. These percentages did not change significantly from the beginning to the end of their teachers education programs.

Beliefs about the use of Uniform Standards for all Students

The problematic character of helping teachers think about issues of equity is illustrated by the responses of teachers in the TELT sample to the statement that 'teachers should use the same standards in evaluating the work of all students in the class (Figure 7.10)'. We included this item because the 'self-fulfilling prophecy' — the idea that students perform up to whatever standard their teachers and others in their environment hold for them — is standard fare in teacher education. Educational psychology courses and textbooks are apparently incomplete without at least passing attention to Rosenthal's 'Pygmalion' research (Rosenthal and Jacobsen, 1968; for a summary of related research, see Dusek, 1985; for a critical review, see Wineburg, 1987) or summaries of research on teachers expectations such as Good and Brophy (1991) offer. In addition, parents of children of colour have become increasingly concerned in recent years about the expectations that teachers, most of whom are white, hold for their children.

Another dimension of this issue is the way in which teachers appear to think about dealing with differences in the classroom. As we found in the TELT and related studies, many practising and prospective teachers seemed to believe that part of being sensitive and responsive to children was by individualizing instruction to address the needs they believe particular students have (McDiarmid and Price, 1990). Individualizing instruction appears to include adapting expectations to individual children. To many teachers, however, this may not constitute 'lowering' expectations but rather tailoring them. Attending to differences in children's understanding, explicitly and directly trying to build students' self-esteem by setting 'attainable' goals, and establishing standards that are 'appropriate' and motivating for particular children is a theme that also appears in educational psychology courses and texts and in various multicultural courses and workshops (McDiarmid, 1990).

As Figure 7.10 reveals, most *preservice teachers* in the TELT sample began their programs believing that 'teachers should use the same standards in evaluating the work of all students in the class'. By the end of their programs, fewer agreed with the statement although the difference was not

G. Williamson McDiarmid

Figure 7.10: Means of Teachers' Responses at the Beginning and End of Preservice, Induction, Alternate Route and Inservice Programs to the Statement: *'Teachers should use the same standards in evaluating the work of all students in the class'*.

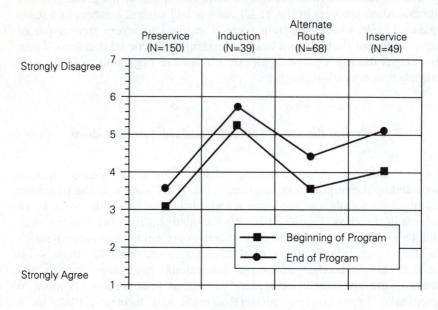

Significance of Change

Preservice	Induction	Alternate Route	Inservice
n.s.	p < .05	p < .01	n.s.

statistically significant. Teachers in the *induction program* sample were significantly different from the preservice teachers at the beginning of their program; few agreed with the idea of applying uniform standards to all students. Teachers in this particular sample, you may remember, had just completed their preservice professional programs and had begun to teach under the eye of a clinical teacher. During their program a statistically significant proportion of the teachers seemed to change their views — or rather, seemed to have become more convinced that teachers should not use the same standards for all students.

A similar change seemed to have occurred among some participants in the *alternate route programs*. Most agreed with the idea of using the same standards for all students at the beginning of their program. By the end, significantly fewer agreed. Most *inservice teachers* disagreed with the statement at the outset and the mean increased by the end of the programs, indicating a change but one that was not statistically significant.

Although teachers in the preservice and inservice programs did not

136

appear to change their views significantly, those in the induction and alternate route programs did. In all cases, however, the direction of change, whether significant or not, was in the same direction; towards disagreeing with the application of uniform standards to all children.

Summary

Several points emerge from the data presented here. We found no instances in which a majority of the teachers in any of the program types seemed to change their minds dramatically — that is, from strongly agreeing to strongly disagreeing — on any of the items designed to tap their beliefs about learners. A 'large' change on an item was in the range of a single point on a seven point-scale. At the same time, however, we found statistically significant differences on a number of the items presented here. Many of these changes represented instances in which teachers had become more convinced or less convinced about the views they held at the outset of their programs. For instance, increased proportions of preservice and induction teachers in the sample appeared to have come to believe that mathematical ability is not entirely innate. This change is correlated with a change in these teachers' views of their own capacities to do mathematics, suggesting the possibility that changes in the views of others may be related to changes in views of themselves.

Most teachers in the sample did not appear to change their belief that ethnic stereotypes represent valid bases on which to make instructional decisions. This appeared as true of those program types that focused particular attention on teachers' knowledge of racially and ethnically diverse learners as it was of program types that afford these issues less attention. Finally, in all but the preservice programs, most teachers believed that teachers should not apply uniform standards in evaluating the work of all students. In general, teachers in our sample appeared to move toward this position during the time they participated in formal teacher education programs.

Discussion

Beliefs about Ability in Mathematics and Writing and their Relation to Gender

Most teachers — whether preservice, induction, alternate route or inservice — seemed to discount the idea that ability in mathematics and writing is principally innate and related to gender. At the same time, most teachers — except for those in the induction program — seemed somewhat lukewarm in their belief that ability is not simply innate. Presented with a statement that cast the idea of natural ability in a positive light ('some people are naturally able to organize their thoughts for writing'), they agreed overwhelmingly.

One interpretation of these data is that teachers know that viewing ability as innate or gender-related is simply socially unacceptable. Encounters with formal teacher education programs emphasize the social and political impalpability of such views and the orthodoxy of the opposing views. Consequently, at the end of these programs, teachers are more likely to disagree with statements that imply that intellectual ability is innate or gender-related regardless of what they genuinely believe.

Another interpretation is that teachers at all levels — preservice through inservice — are suspicious of assertions that ability in mathematics and writing is innate; their experiences in formal teacher education programs and in classrooms, serve to confirm these suspicions. Yet this interpretation, like the one above, does not account for the large proportion of teachers who indicated they were unsure about the gender-relatedness of ability. Nearly a quarter of the samples in each program chose the 'not sure' option for the statement about the need for a 'mathematical mind'.

Such levels of uncertainty may be due to the teachers' awareness of the conflicting results reported by various researchers who study sex differences in mathematics achievement as measured on standardized tests. That boys score better on such measures of mathematics after the middle grades in elementary school seems undeniable. For instance, Benbow and Stanley (1980) found that among mathematically gifted seventh graders, twice as many boys as girls scored above 500 on the mathematics section of the SAT. Yet, researchers disagree on the sources of the substantial differences in mathematical achievement between the sexes. Some argue that differences result from social factors while others contend that physiological differences underlie the gaps in achievement (Armstrong, 1975; Benbow and Stanley, 1980; Fenemma, 1975; Leinhardt, Seewald and Engel, 1979).

Much of this research, however, takes as a given that standardized tests are valid measures of mathematical ability when, in fact, these tests are designed to measure mathematical achievement (Rudisall and Morrison, 1989). Awareness of what standardized tests do and do not measure might contribute further to teachers' uncertainties about issues of sex differences and the degree to which ability is malleable.

Unfortunately, our data do not allow us to decide which of these interpretations best fits with how teachers in the sample think about the issues. At the same time, our finding that changes in teachers' beliefs about their own capacity to do mathematics are correlated positively with changes in their beliefs about the capacity of others to do mathematics is intriguing. This finding suggests that teachers who reassess their beliefs about themselves as learners may also reassess others as learners. In those programs in which significant beginning-to-end differences occurred for the item on one's own capacity to do advanced mathematics, differences on the 'mathematical mind' item also occurred. This is, however, merely associational; whether the link between views of the self and others is causal, though intuitively appealing, remains to be demonstrated.

Beliefs about Sources of School Success and Failure

The results we have presented lend themselves to several interpretations. That so many teachers believe that students' attitude is the primary source of their success is not surprising in a society that places such emphasis on individual achievement. Moreover, educators have touted enhanced 'self-esteem' as the cure for student failure, particularly among poor children and those of colour. Responses to this item may reflect the degree to which those who advocate 'enhanced self-esteem' have been successful in convincing others that self-regard operates and can be developed independently of academic accomplishment. Or responses may reflect a common-sense notion of the role that student enthusiasm and perseverance play in success and failure, a notion captured in the old saw: 'you can lead a horse to water but you can't make him drink'. Finally, as several teachers pointed out, attempting to assign student success and failure to any single predominant factor is an artificial exercise; a combination of factors, some related more to the students and others related more to the teacher, that are themselves inter-related, determine success or failure.

None the less, that half or fewer of the teachers in all program types but one chose teacher factors as the most frequent sources of student failure may concern teacher educators. In some schools, teachers inclined to look for reasons to explain why students don't learn more can find them readily at hand — in what they perceive as students' indifference or resistance, lack of support in the home, impoverished conditions in the community, and so on. Yet, teachers manifestly have moral and legal obligations to teach, regardless of these conditions. That many may believe that student failure, to a considerable extent, is outside of their control is worrisome. We cannot, however, be sure this is what teachers intended by their responses.

Beliefs about Stereotypes of Others

Unlike the questionnaire items discussed above, this item is one for which we gathered considerable interview data. The results are, again, somewhat worrisome. When presented with what was clearly a stereotype of native American students, only about half of the preservice and alternate route teachers in our samples, at the end of their teacher education programs, questioned the validity of such information for making instructional decisions. Accepting stereotypes as valid information for teaching is worrying even when the stereotype is positive or neutral because such acceptance may signal an inclination to prejudge students on the basis of their membership in a particular ethnic group.

These findings are particularly troubling because of what we have learned about how issues of diversity are treated in some programs (McDiarmid, 1990; McDiarmid and Price, 1990). On the one hand, teachers are exhorted to treat all children the same; on the other, they are urged to attend to each child's uniqueness, to each child's cultural heritage. Understandably, teachers express confusion about how they are to treat children who are socially, ethnically and culturally different from themselves. This uncertainty may be reflected in responses to this scenario. Between a quarter and a half of the teachers in the sample declared themselves unsure about how to treat the stereotype or gave answers in which they seemed, at some points in the interview, to accept the stereotype and, at others, reject it. This uncertainty increased between the beginning and end of their teacher education programs.

Beliefs about the Use of Uniform Standards in Evaluating Student Performance

On this issue we found substantial differences among teachers in the sample — and differences within programs between the beginning and end. Those in the induction and inservice programs strongly disagreed with the idea of uniform standards while those in the preservice programs agreed. At the same time, the general tendency was for teachers to disagree with uniform standards more at the end of their programs than they did at the beginning. Is this, however, a positive outcome for their students? Is such a view likely to lead to better opportunities to learn for students, especially poor and minority children?

From one perspective, such a change in teachers' beliefs could be regarded as problematic; holding children from groups that have been historically denied equitable opportunities to learn to lower standards merely perpetuates their second class status in schools. Ensuring that these children experience success in school, experience themselves as people capable of doing what is required of them in school, is, arguably, equally critical. So, does this trend we found in the data promise better opportunities to learn for these children or just more of the same?

Faculty and personnel in the various programs appear to disagree about this issue themselves. The predominant view of those who work in the inservice and alternate route programs appears to be that teachers should not hold all students to the same standard while the majority view among faculty in preservice programs appears to be that they should (Tatto, Kennedy, and Schmidt, in press).

Given the debate over teacher expectations, what information is likely to be helpful to teachers? And what is most critical for teachers: information derived from various research on the effects of teacher expectations and 'attainable' goals on poor and minority children or the opportunity to consider and discuss the issue in the context of an actual classroom situation? The programs in our sample seem to have elected the former but whether this best serves teachers and, ultimately, children remains unanswered.

Conclusion

In spite of problems with the TELT data, several themes emerge from the analysis presented here. The first is that on a number of issues that have to do with learners, the views of teachers in different types of programs were divided. This should serve as an antidote to broad generalization about what teachers think. Secondly, some teachers in the sample, enrolled in various types of programs, did appear to change their minds about learner's capacities — and their own — while they were involved in formal teacher education programs. In most cases, the changes were not dramatic; teachers rarely appeared to change their minds completely — that is, disagreeing with statements at the end of their program with which they had initially agreed. Rather, they appeared to become more or less convinced about a given issue.

None the less, these findings may challenge the charge that both critics and teachers themselves frequently level: that little or no learning occurs in teacher education. These data do not, of course, reveal which opportunities in the programs influence teachers' beliefs about learners. Practical experiences, for instance, are part of each of the programs in the sample and these could be, as teachers often claim they are, the most influential aspect of the programs.

As to their beliefs about learners, most teachers, by the end of their programs, seemed to be less sure that ability in mathematics or writing is innate and gender related. Intriguingly, changes in teachers' beliefs about the capacities of others to do mathematics seemed to be associated with changes in their beliefs about their own capacity to do mathematics. Whether these beliefs are causally related remains to be determined.

At the same time, most think that students' attitudes are the primary source of their success or failure in school although a number of teachers complete their teacher education programs with a new appreciation for the role of the teacher in student failure. Although many teachers did not question the validity of a stereotype as a basis for classroom decisions, a sizeable proportion were uncertain about the issue. Finally, teachers appeared divided on the issue of evaluating all students by the same standards.

On a number of these issues, whether one regards the results as positive or negative depends on one's own beliefs about learners and about what teachers need to know and believe. For instance, if one believes that holding all learners to the same standards is the best way to ensure that historically under-served students will learn more, then one will be cheered by the beliefs of the preservice and alternate route teachers and dismayed by those of the induction teachers. On other issues, such as the role of generalizations about learners in making classroom decisions, the results may well concern everyone because of the high levels of uncertainty they reveal. Many teachers aren't sure how to treat generalized information about learners culturally different from themselves and the teacher education programs in the TELT sample did not seem to help them become clearer on this issue.

Acknowledgments

The author gratefully acknowledges the assistance of Jaime Grinberg who conducted the computer analyses of the data on which this paper is based. Preparation of this paper was supported by the National Center for Research on Teacher Learning, Michigan State University and the College of Education, Michigan State University. The NCRTL is funded by the Office of Educational Research and Improvement, United States Department of Education and by the College of Education, Michigan State University. The opinions expressed herein are those of the author and do not necessarily reflect the position, policy or endorsement of the College of Education or OERI/ED. (Grant No. OERI-G-86-0001).

References

ARMSTRONG, J.R. (1975) 'Factors in intelligence and mathematical ability which may account for differences in mathematics achievement between the sexes', in FENEMMA, E. (ed.) *Mathematics learning: What research says about sex differences*, ERIC Document Reproduction Service No. ED 128 195.

BENBOW, C.P. and STANLEY, J.C. (1980) 'Sex differences in mathematical ability: Fact or artifact?' *Science*, **210**, pp. 1262–4.

DUSEK, J.B. (1985) *Teacher expectancies*, Hillsdale, NJ: Lawrence Erlbaum.

FENEMMA, E. (1975) 'Mathematics, spatial ability and the sexes', in FENEMMA, E. (ed.) *Mathematics learning: What research says about sex differences*, ERIC Document Reproduction Service No. ED 128 195.

GOOD, T.L. and BROPHY, J.E. (1991) *Looking in classrooms*, (5th edition), New York: Harper Collins.

HAWKINS, D. (1974) 'I, thou, and it', in Hawkins, D. *The informed vision: Essays on learning and human nature*, New York: Agathon Press, pp. 48–62.

KENNEDY, M.M., BALL, D.L., McDIARMID, G.W. and SCHMIDT, W. (in press) *The Teacher Education and Learning to Teach Study: A guide to studying teacher education programs* (Technical Series), E. Lansing, MI: Michigan State University, National Center for Research on Teacher Education.

KERR, D.H. (1981) 'The structure of quality in teaching', in SOLTIS, J. (ed.) *Philosophy and education: Eightieth yearbook of the National Society for the Study of Education*, Chicago: University of Chicago, pp. 61–93.

LEINHARDT, G., SEEWALD, A.M. and ENGEL, M. (1979) 'Learning what's taught: Sex differences in instruction, *Journal of Educational Psychology*, **71**, pp. 432–9.

MCDIARMID, G.W. (1990) *What to do about differences? A study of multicultural education for teacher trainees in the Los Angeles Unified School District*, (Research Report No. 90-11), E. Lansing, MI: Michigan State University, National Center for Research on Teacher Education.

MCDIARMID, G.W. and BALL, D.L. (1989) *The Teacher Education and Learning to Teach Study: An occasion for developing a conception of teacher knowledge* (Technical Series No. 89-1), E. Lansing, MI: Michigan State University, National Center for Research on Teacher Education.

MCDIARMID, G.W. and PRICE, J. (1990) *Prospective teachers' views of diverse learners: A study of the participants in the ABCD project* (Research report No. 90-6), E. Lansing, MI: Michigan State University, National Center for Research on Teacher Education.

NATIONAL RESEARCH COUNCIL (1989) *Everybody Counts: A report to the Nation on the Future of Mathematics Education*, Washington, D.C.: National Academy Press.

ROSENTHAL, R. and JACOBSON, L. (1968) *Pygmalion in the classroom*, New York: Holt Reinhart, Winston.

RUDISALL, E.M. and MORRISON, L.J. (1989) 'Sex differences in mathematics achievement: An emerging case for physiological factors', *School Science and Mathematics*, **89**(7), pp. 571–7.

SCHWAB, J.J. (1960/1978) Education and the structure of the disciplines', in WESTBURY, I. and WILKOF, N. (eds), *Science, curriculum, and liberal education: Selected essays*, Chicago: University of Chicago Press, pp. 229–72.

TATTO, M.T., KENNEDY, M.M. and SCHMIDT, W. (in press) *Understanding the core of teacher education: An analysis of faculty, experienced and prospective teachers' views of teaching, learning, and learning to teach*, E. Lansing, MI: Michigan State University, National Center for Research on Teacher Education.

WINEBURG, S.S. (1987) 'The self-fulfillment of the self-fulfilling prophecy: A critical appraisal', *Educational Researcher*, **16**(9), pp. 28–37.

8   Critical Attributes of a Reflective Teacher: Is Agreement Possible?

Tom Russell

The issue of the role of 'reflection' in teacher development brings together researchers from a wide variety of backgrounds and, accordingly, a wide variety of perspectives on what reflection is and could be in teacher education. It will be difficult to detect actual effects of increasing attention to reflection in teacher development while the term 'reflection' means so many things to so many people. Is agreement possible, desirable, or necessary for further progress in teacher education? The following questions indicate some areas of potential differences in opinion with respect to the place of reflection in teacher education and development.

- How does a teacher know when reflection is productive?
- How does an observer recognize a reflective teacher?
- Is a reflective teacher a good teacher?
- How is a weak reflective teacher different from a strong un-reflective teacher?
- Can a teacher whose practices never change be said to be reflective?
- Is a teacher who can articulate principles of practice being reflective?
- Does being reflective mean thinking about one's teaching, or does it also require doing something about one's teaching?
- Can one be a reflective teacher while denying all interest in reflection?

There are many questions that can be posed with respect to use of the term 'reflection' in the context of teaching and teacher education. The questions in the preceding list are posed for a general audience that has not worked extensively with a specialized meaning for 'reflection'. It should be acknowledged, however, that it is my work with one of the most recent specialized terms — Schön's (1983) 'reflection-in-action' — that forms the backdrop to these questions and the responses given below. The list of questions is not intended to be an exhaustive list, but it has been found useful in generating productive discussion about reflection and teaching. Increasing attention to reflection during the 1980s has generated a new literature (Calderhead, 1988, and Schön, 1991, are but two examples) of teacher development that raises questions and new frames much more rapidly than initial teacher education courses can respond. This new literature challenges all teacher educators to better understand their personal assumptions about reflection and learning to teach. The questions above suggest areas in which teacher educators need to understand better their similarities and differences — in theory and in action — if, working individually and collectively, they are to make a significant contribution to fostering teacher development through reflection.

This chapter was first developed during a sabbatical leave in a university department of education in England during the 1990–91 academic year. Spending a year in the context of different perspectives and practices was invaluable in extending my own use of the term 'reflection', in my writing and in my observations of those learning to teach. To develop the argument of this chapter, each of my opening questions is briefly discussed. The responses to the questions reveal some of my own assumptions about reflection in teacher development, and I suggest that each teacher educator and researcher can better understand personal assumptions about reflection by responding to these questions. To complete the argument, I turn to the question of how we conceptualize the role of reflection in the development of the 'weak' student teacher whose performance in teaching practice seems marginal. I contend that any conceptualization of reflection in teacher development that is minimally adequate must help us better understand and be of assistance to the student teacher or beginning teacher for whom learning to teach is a difficult, confusing and frustrating experience.

Questioning Reflection and Reflective Practice

How Does a Teacher Know when Reflection is Productive?

In common-sense terms, we often feel we are not being reflective enough and wish that we had 'more time' for reflection about the things we do. I am inclined to think that most teachers would be reflective most of the time in an appropriate and supportive school environment. Unfortunately, many school environments do not support a reflective stance toward professional practice, so that the importance of the on-going 'mulling over' of each lesson's events is often obscured. Nor are teachers regularly encouraged to take advantages of the available opportunities to act on hunches and generally achieve the new understandings that result from making changes (large or small) in their teaching. As in the culture generally, so it is in the school culture: we have been persuaded that new and improved knowledge is gained from external sources and 'experts' rather than from personal experience, by listening rather than by acting. A short response to this question could be 'Reflection is productive when it leads to changes in practice that may or may not be retained but that result in a better personal understanding of one's practice'.

How Does an Observer Recognize a Reflective Teacher?

'Only by investing considerable time in observation and discussion'. Recognizing a reflective teacher is certainly not a matter of concluding that a teacher is good or effective by observing a single lesson with a checklist of desirable behaviours. To assess the extent to which a teacher is reflective about practice may require observation of several lessons, with subsequent conversation about each, with a view to listening for puzzles and dilemmas, for re-thinking of assumptions and beliefs, and for evidence that these are taken into the practice setting. Changes in practice do not have to be successful; rather, one needs to consider why particular changes were or were not successful and why the benefits outweigh the costs if changes are retained.

Is a Reflective Teacher a Good Teacher?

'Not necessarily'. If one had the deliberate intention of being a poor teacher, the attributes of the reflective teacher could be very helpful in ensuring that one achieved that (unlikely) goal. I pose this question because teacher education and research on teaching has such a long history of seeking to identify characteristics that distinguish good from poor teachers, more effective from less effective. It is almost inevitable that if both reflection and good teaching are seen as desirable, they will be seen as related, yet I believe we are more likely to understand reflection if we keep it separate from the elusive and time-worn issue of what represents 'good' teaching.

How is a Weak Reflective Teacher Different from a Strong Un-reflective Teacher?

Here there is no simple reply. The question is important because we are predisposed to assume that being reflective and being successful go hand in hand. We must be particularly cautious about such assumptions, recalling how easy it is to express in speech and in writing very impressive views about teaching and learning but to display 'ordinary' teaching behaviours when observed by others. There are at least three issues involved here: quality of teaching (as perceived by pupils and by observers), quality of reflection (based on spoken and written words and on observations of practice), and consistency — the extent to which one's teaching practice matches one's beliefs and self-perceptions. We want a strong teacher to be reflective, but we also want reflection to help a weak teacher to become stronger. 'Reflection' has long been a desirable characteristic among teacher educators, but a cogent account of how reflection facilitates improvement has been lacking.

Can a Teacher Whose Practices Never Change be said to be Reflective?

Here the easiest reply is 'probably not'. On the premise that reflection requires on-going scrutiny of practice while rejecting the easy assumption that one is doing what one thinks one is doing, practices need to be changed for several reasons. The enterprise of teaching seems to be one that can never be taken for granted and never fully understood. Dilemmas of some sort are always present. We need to make changes in our practices both to see if better compromises can be achieved and to understand better what we think we are doing.

Is a Teacher who can Articulate Principles of Practice being Reflective?

'Yes', if the principles of practice match the practice rather than personal beliefs about the practice. Through many years of schooling, we may become quite vocal about how we think good teachers should teach. Thus we may be able to articulate principles with little or no understanding of what it means to express them in practice. One result is that it is far too easy to believe that one is expressing one's beliefs in one's teaching, even to believe that this is the meaning of 'putting theory into practice'. Those who have observed teachers at length and worked to compare beliefs with actual practices, tend to be very aware of the significant gaps between beliefs and actions. Many teacher educators are interested in the processes of reflection for their potential to reduce the gaps between thought and action.

Does Being Reflective Mean Thinking about One's Teaching, or Does it also Require Doing Something about One's Teaching?

Here we find a significant area for potential differences of opinion. A personal interest in Schön's (1983) explication of 'reflection-in-action' leads me to the potentially 'extreme' position that being reflective serves little purpose if it does not involve, in central and essential ways, changes to teaching as well as development of thinking about teaching. Every aspect of teaching that can be thought about becomes far more complex at the level of practice.

Tom Russell

> *Can One be a Reflective Teacher while Denying All Interest in Reflection?*

Here again, it seems possible but improbable. Denial of interest in reflection would, in most instances, be driven by some larger issue, perhaps quite unrelated to the process of reflection. Teachers tend not to talk about how they learned to teach; teaching practice and the first years of teaching tend to be exhausting and humbling experience in which we are largely on our own. Reflection is associated with academic activities, yet one may resent that one's academic program did not seem to provide better preparation for the demands of teaching practice and the first year or two of teaching.

Can Reflection Help the Weak Teacher Improve?

The opportunity to see teacher education in a new context, with variations on familiar traditions and political pressures, during a year-long sabbatical leave, created an important opportunity to rethink basic assumptions about teacher education — my personal assumptions and those embedded in our academic traditions and current practices. Early in my work in initial teacher education I had noticed that despite our wishes and intentions to help the weak student teacher improve, progress seemed very difficult for those who do not experience success early in their practicum experiences. Conversations with tutors and students on a PGCE course and visits to schools (one day each week) in the autumn term and during the extended practicum in the spring term stimulated many new perspectives on existing practices of teacher education. I believe I am beginning to understand why it is so difficult to help the weak beginning teacher. (Russell *et al.*, 1988, gives an account of the research, carried out with my colleague Hugh Munby, that serves as a background to this analysis.)

We assume that beginners learn to teach by being told how to teach. This is the underlying premise in our teaching activities in the university setting and in our post-observation conversations during assessment of practicum performance. We also assume that practical experience in schools leads directly to learning how to teach (Edwards and Mercer, 1987, offer data and arguments that challenge this assumption). We assume that the introduction to teaching experience should be gradual, and we assume that all experiences in schools are educative for student teachers. Overall, and understandably, we take for granted that we do adequately understand how people learn to teach and that these understandings are expressed in the structures of our courses.

My opportunity to reflect on my own practices in Canada while observing and inquiring about practices in England has led me to realize that there are interesting differences in such features as length of practicum experience, commentary provided to beginners by experienced teachers and tutors, and practices for assessing success in initial teaching. When I consider these differences, I can see the shared beliefs that sustain the variations. I am also moved to the conclusion that our conceptualization of learning to teach is as inadequate as our interpretations of reflection are diverse. The two issues seem related in important ways.

Quite universally, student teachers describe the practicum as the most important and valuable activity among the various activities associated with learning to teach. I have long accepted this conclusion that we learn from experience, a conclusion that is also embedded in the reality that some teachers teach without formal training, including most of those appointed to university teaching posts. At the same time, I have tried to understand better what contribution is made by the spoken word — in university classrooms and lecture halls and in the commentaries offered to beginners by experienced teachers who observe them. These efforts are often less than satisfying, but I manage to sustain a belief that what I do is valuable.

My own interpretation of 'reflection' is that it is closely related to learning from experience, the aspect of learning to teach that we least understand. What happens if we assume that experience is the essential source of learning to teach and that most of what we do with words (spoken and written) is of no more than marginal impact? Could this be the case without our being aware of it? On reflection, evidence to contradict the value of verbal and written activities is easily hidden. We believe, after all, in the value of verbal and written communication, and learning by experience is only poorly understood. Most student teachers are very successful at listening and responding, and have well-developed skills (from years of practice as students) for finding some meaning and value in any classroom experience in which they play a student role. Also, most beginners seem to develop adequate teaching performances quite quickly — learning from experience if the assumption I have suggested is followed. If we see them improving day by day, week by week, and if these improvements are accompanied by our occasional visits to observe and offer suggestions, we would readily conclude that spoken words are helping them learn to teach, even if they were not, for their teaching performances are improving. At the same time, endowed by schooling with the same faith in learning through speech and writing, beginners themselves seek the verbal and written comments of experienced teachers and believe the comments help them learn to teach.

It is the case of the weak student teacher that should be the source of evidence for questioning our faith in learning from words. The weak student teacher seems very slow to learn from experience. The criticisms and suggestions we offer, in good faith and with belief in verbal learning, seem to have little effect in enabling the weak teacher to improve. Rather than questioning our medium of communication or our assumptions about how one learns to teach, we conclude that the weak student teacher 'failed to take the advice' offered by teachers and tutors. Ultimately, a few drop out or fail, and we conclude that they were 'not cut out to be teachers'; our premises remain intact. Why is it so easy to fault the student who learns slowly, the student for whom it is not enough to use the processes that seem to be effective with those who progress quickly? Admittedly, the weak student teacher is inconvenient in an administrative sense, awkward in terms of relations with the host school, and frustrating when more time is requested for visits and assessment of progress.

An alternative interpretation (that I intend to pursue at the level of action) begins with the assumption that the weak student teacher who does not respond to advice is less able to learn quickly from initial practicum experiences. Consider just how quickly a student teacher becomes a liability and source of frustration to the teachers and school when classes go poorly and pupils begin to fall behind. There is little opportunity or support for 'learning how to learn from experience' over an extended period, particularly in a time frame as short as two weeks, which is the standard length of a teaching placement in the program in which I work in Ontario. When a PGCE student on a ten-week placement invited me to observe his teaching, it seemed that a unique opportunity had been offered to test my assumptions in the context of practice. The invitation was extended by the student teacher just after the half-term break, when his failure to show improvement had led the school to reduce his weekly teaching responsibilities to three hour-long classes with a single set of pupils. I observed three lessons out of a series of five, including two consecutive lessons. Observing two consecutive lessons (never possible in my Ontario time frame), each followed immediately by tape-recorded discussion, led to the understanding of the student teacher's performance and personal sense of that performance, far richer and far more detailed than the understanding I have come to associate with an isolated visit, possibly followed by further visits at intervals of several weeks. Time for extended conversation with the regular teacher (who also sat in on the lessons I observed but was not present for the discussions) revealed to me the patience that was being displayed by the teacher and the trust that this patience inspired in the student teacher.

While I gained very valuable opportunities to re-think my assumptions about learning to teach, in the final analysis the student teacher was judged to have failed the teaching practice. No decision of failure is arrived at without due process, and in this instance the relevant data (from the perspectives of the tutor, the practicum school, and an external examiner) converged clearly on the conclusion of unsuccessful performance and failure to accept the most basic advice. Here my background in another teacher education context became a liability, for a student teacher who failed would invariably be offered another opportunity, making a fresh start in a different school. Ironically, it was only at the very end of my stay in England that I became aware of relevant data that could have modified radically my own efforts to be of assistance. The student teacher had many years of experience in a science-based industrial context and an impressive practical knowledge of aspects of one of the familiar school science subjects. In Canada, no student teacher could complete a program of initial teacher education without also completing an undergraduate degree, and I never imagined that this student teacher's formal education might have ended with his A-level studies. This new information helped me reinterpret my observations from the perspective that the individual in question lacked the university-based view of the subject that the school curriculum takes so completely for granted. Here was further reason to see that the failure to act on advice was driven by fundamental differences in perception between those who offered the advice and the individual attempting to improve his teaching.

My conclusion from this intense involvement with a failure to learn to teach is that the weak student teacher needs much more help than we normally offer in how to reflect on his/her teaching — on how to consider events of teaching in fine detail and to plan for modest and attainable changes that could gradually produce improvements not only in performance and confidence, but also in an understanding of how different aspects of classroom activities relate and interact. One can attempt to tackle management directly and in isolation, with lists of tips and suggestions, but issues of management are usually linked closely to pace, coherent directions, and an organization of content that suits the perspectives of the pupils. The student teacher who succeeds at the outset, or who improves quickly, could be said to learn this close linkage from experience, quite rapidly and quite possibly without realizing it. The student teacher who improves slowly or not at all could be said to be experiencing difficulties in perceiving how a host of elements of teaching interact to produce a teaching performance that maintains order and attention while enabling students to interact with the required content at a reasonable pace.

I believe that reflection plays a vital role in teacher development, and I believe that instances of weak or slow-to-succeed teachers are the most important test of that belief. I believe that reflection is closely linked to learning from experience rather than from spoken and written advice, but that learning from experience is neglected in traditional practices of teacher education, across all international boundaries. I am not suggesting that verbal advice is of no help, only that it appears to be of little help until one is successful at learning from experience. Our efforts to identify critical attributes of a reflective teacher, and to find ways to develop those attributes among those for whom getting better at teaching is slow, difficult and frustrating, have the potential to move us closer to an adequate understanding of how individuals learn to teach and to improve their teaching over the course of a career.

Is Agreement Possible?

Agreement about the nature and role of reflection in teaching and learning to teach will not come easily, but with time, patience and effort, greater agreement may be possible. I have not simplified the prospects for agreement by raising the further challenge that our conceptualization of reflection in teacher development should be tested against the perennial problem of helping the weak beginning teacher to improve. At the same time, by posing that challenge and linking reflection with learning from experience, I may suggest to some that I would favour relocating initial teacher education from the universities to the schools — a proposal that is being advanced in the UK at this time by critics of existing teacher education practices and results. Nothing could be more inappropriate, for it is the role of the university in our society to inquire into assumptions and develop alternative interpretations. But teacher education does not have an impressive record of such activities. (Rudduck (1992) identifies important flaws in the let-the-schools-train-the-teachers view and describes one structural approach to fostering reflection by beginning teachers. Richert (1992) shows that different structures for reflection yield significantly different types of reflection.)

New frames for teacher education, inspired in part by efforts to agree on critical attributes of reflective teachers, are more likely to emerge in the university than in the schools where student teachers practice, although there is little indication that we are very far along that path. What I would favour is a great deal of thoughtful experimentation in our initial teacher education courses. This would include efforts to develop reflection — learning from experience — by beginning teachers. It would also include more time in which tutors worked more closely with beginning teachers in their host schools, working to understand better (and to enable the beginner to understand better) how experience and verbal commentaries contribute to learning to teach. If we can begin to be of more help to those who find learning to teach most difficult, then we will better understand what are the critical attributes of a reflective teacher.

It would be very satisfying to conclude with a detailed account of how individual teachers learn from experience, whether they learn quickly or slowly, whether they succeed or fail in teaching practice. Such an account remains a long-term, possibly elusive, personal goal. My efforts to work with Schön's account of reflection-in-action have been encouraging. In this chapter I have focused on our assumptions about the process of learning to teach. It is increasingly clear that our assumptions, pervasive yet unacknowledged and unexamined, make development of accounts of learning from experience complex and problematic. Those who are learning to teach and those who are working to facilitate that learning, hold assumptions that mask the important details of learning from experience. The student teacher who learns slowly and with difficulty seems most likely to offer opportunities to identify existing assumptions and to test alternatives associated more directly with learning from experience.

References

CALDERHEAD, J. (ed.) (1988) *Teachers' Professional Learning*, Lewes: Falmer Press.

EDWARDS, D. and MERCER, N. (1987) *Common Knowledge: The Development of Understanding in the Classroom*, London: Routledge.

RICHERT, A.E. (1992) 'The Content of Student Teachers' Reflections within Different Structures for Facilitating the Reflective Process', in RUSSELL, T. and MUNBY, H. (eds) *Teachers and Teaching: From Classroom to Reflection*, London: Falmer Press, pp. 171–91.

RUDDUCK, J. (1992) 'Practitioner Research and Programmes of Initial Teacher Education', in RUSSELL, T. and MUNBY, H. (eds) *Teachers and Teaching: From Classroom to Reflection*, London: Falmer Press, pp. 156–70.

RUSSELL, T., MUNBY, H., JOHNSTON, P. and SPAFFORD, C. (1988) 'Learning the Professional Knowledge of Teaching: Metaphors, Puzzles, and the Theory-Practice Relationship', in GRIMMETT, P.P. and ERICKSON, G.L. (eds) *Reflection in Teacher Education*, New York, Teachers College Press, pp. 67–90.

SCHÖN, D.A. (1983) *The Reflective Practitioner: How Professionals Think in Action*, New York: Basic Books.

— (ed.) (1991) *The Reflective Turn: Case studies in and on Educational Practice*, New York: Teachers College Press.

9   Supporting Reflection in Teachers' Learning

Anne Edwards and *David Brunton*

We would hazard that most B.Ed. and PGCE programmes in the UK contain the aim 'to produce the reflective practitioner'. Equally there is a proliferation of courses for practitioners which encourage reflective teaching. The recent UK Department of Education and Science (DES) 'task force' report (DES, 1990) implicitly accepts that the way forward for the inservice education of teachers (INSET) is consideration of self in context. Yet it may be that the complexities of the reflective process are lost in the ubiquity of notions of quality, considered action and self-evaluation. It is therefore our intention to focus upon some of these complexities and to consider the ways in which external change-agents can sponsor and support the development of reflective practitioners.

Within the context of INSET, Day's (1985) discussion of the ways in which teachers learn, and the role of the researcher as intervenor, is extremely helpful in explaining the processes of creating contexts for adult learning and the important role that the INSET provider may assume as that is undertaken. As financial constraints determine a shift to more school-based INSET work with an increased load on internal staff development support systems, it may be timely to examine those processes which relate to adult learning and ultimately to the application of new skills and understanding. If schools increasingly and creatively explore new ways of supporting staff development and integrating it into strategies for improving the quality of provision, then an understanding of how 'reflection on' may relate to 'learning about' and 'application of' new professional skills will be crucial.

This understanding demands a consideration of the possibilities for personal reflection, professional growth and extended competence within programmes which are designed to achieve the multiple goals of curriculum development and organizational improvement. We would suggest that an understanding of the processes of professional learning within such developmental strategies is as important as a concern for teacher esteem for anyone involved in supporting teachers' learning. Such work may take place through institutional development planning, collaborative INSET programmes, strategies of supported self-evaluation, or staff appraisal systems.

Our starting point is to take seriously the processes of action research (Hopkins, 1985) and to recognize their importance in terms of teacher thinking and learning as well as the development of the school as an organization. Much of the justification of action research has focused on the latter, whether explicitly relating it to organizational development (Hopkins, 1989) or connecting it to models of empowerment and social justice (Carr and Kemmis, 1986). While we would want to acknowledge and draw upon this work, our concerns are more in tune with those of Day (1985), as we explore the processes of reflection central to action research and their relationship to teachers' learning.

The model of learning to which we subscribe is Vygotskian in origin. It is one which recognizes developmental processes which are 'deeply rooted in the links between individual and social history' (Vygotsky, 1978) and the role of the 'other' or mediator in learning. 'Even the competent adult can profit from regulation for enhancement and maintenance of performance' (Tharp and Gallimore, 1991). This view of learning emphasizes the neo-Vygotskian premise of mediated learning with its consequent recognition of the goal-directedness of learner and mediator. The importance of language and dialogue in cultural transmission and acquisition is also well supported in the literature on learning in both formal and informal settings (Gal'Perin, 1970; Norman, 1978; Bennett, Desforges, Cockburn and Wilkinson, 1984; Wertsch, 1985) and is a topic we will be developing in relation to reflection on practice.

Interestingly, there is little evidence of the explicit applications of the neo-Vygotskian branch of cognitive developmental psychology to the notion of reflective practice and to the role of the mediator as critical friend within that. We assume in our analysis that the critical friend may fulfil any of a number of roles to include: commissioned evaluator, consultant, college tutor, INSET provider, in-house mentor or curriculum coordinator. In each case, there is a commitment to improve the quality of provision for pupils. There is also a complex pedagogical process to manage at each level.

Like Smyth (1988) we are anxious to ensure that practitioners are at the centre of their own learning and that dependency relationships be avoided if teachers are to be empowered as fully effective participants in the discourse of education. Recent research on children's learning (Light and Perret-Clermont, 1991; Walkerdine, 1988) has demonstrated the importance of discourse formats and the use of dialogue as a means of enabling or empowering the learner to enter and participate within the discourses of established fields and study. Here research on language and learning meshes clearly with more traditional notions of action research and practitioner empowerment. Both regard the ability to participate in and hence in someway manage oneself within the discourse to be a first order aim.

Such ambitions are clearly intended to transform the ways in which knowledge about teaching and learning are produced and re-produced. The intention is that teachers should become active agents in the production of a new pedagogic discourse, rather than merely the consumers of the professional knowledge produced by academics and educational researchers. Such an enterprise is at the heart of Carr and Kemmis' concern for critical theory and action research; John Elliott has described these 'theory-practice problems' and asserted that school-based action research can potentially release teachers from the traditional craft culture of schools. However, he also suggests that the involvement of staff from higher education in sponsoring and supporting the development of a new pedagogic discourse based upon practitioner research might result in teachers becoming ensnared in a 'new epistemological hegemony of academe' (Elliott, 1991).

Clearly, issues of dependence and autonomy are central to the role of the external change-agent or critical friend in managing the pedagogical relationship involved in supporting practitioner research and professional growth. It would be an unhappy irony if the philosophies and procedures of action research, driven by their concern for practitioner improvement, effectively produced new forms of professional dependency and domination. We therefore wish to focus upon some of the aspects of the professional learning of teachers, and the implications for the role of supervisor, mentor, critical friend or mediator.

The importance of language in learning has long been recognized. Theories acknowledging the role of language in learning do not imply a static relationship between goal-directed 'expert' teacher/transmitter and 'novice' learner/receiver. Conversely, they recognize shifts in the nature of the interactions at different points in the learning process and corresponding shifts in the control of the language. A brief examination of two similar learning cycles in sympathy with the work of Vygotsky may illustrate the point.

Norman (1978) makes an analysis of task demand as the learning cycle moves the learner through three stages: from work alongside the teacher, to restructuring activities in which the learner makes sense alone or with others by connecting new knowledge to existing cognitive structures, to a final stage in which the learner fine tunes and uses the skills and knowledge in his or her practice. Norman notes that progress through the stages is not directly linear but that there may be a need to return to a previous stage before moving on again within the current one. This progression is matched by Gal'Perin's sequence of learning in which the learner moves through what he has described as five steps. We have adapted Gal'Perin's five stages so that the language is appropriate to describe the professional development of adult learners (Figure 9.1).

In both models there is a fluctuating role for the mediator. At first, dialogue may be driven by the goals of the expert, but a gradual shift towards exercising the intentionality of the learner is apparent. In the middle stages a monitorial role is assumed by the mediator with availability for discussion and clarification; this is then followed by perhaps the facilitation

Figure 9.1: Five Stages in Learning (after Gal'Perin, 1970)

1. Creating a preliminary conception of the action.

2. Taking practical action steps.

3. Talking about the action and its implications.

4. Internalizing the routine and potential implications of the actions.

5. Consolidating understanding through incorporating ideas into practice.

of public self-review or accountability. At each stage dialogue is necessary but varied in purpose. It is also important to recognize that the learning relationship between mediator and practitioner may extend through a number of learning cycles, and in each cycle the forms of supervision and the patterns of interaction between the mediator and practitioner are likely to be managed in different ways.

In action research terms the process may be conceptualized as a move from accepted and incompletely understood practices, to an understanding which allows extrapolation of continuous and active professional hypo-thesizing. An adaptation of Harré's representation of Vygotsky's learning model provides a useful framework which may help us to examine the link between cycles of learning and reflection in and on practice. More specifically it may afford an exploration of the role of the change-agent within that cycle (Figure 9.2).

Within this framework, quadrants A and D represent the public levels of the learning cycle: what Vygotsky referred to as the intermental plane. Quadrants B and C are the private levels, or Vygotsky's intramental plane. Vygotsky explains that learning needs to occur at both planes: first at the intermental or social and then at the intramental or personal. In this way the concerns of the collective or culture are taken on by the individual (Vygotsky, 1991).

This may be related back to the research of both Norman and Gal'Perin, as work alongside others occurs in A when tasks and goals are negotiated at the social and collective levels. Attempts at restructuring and making connections to existing personal constructions or understanding occur in B, while moves towards internalization and new understanding takes place at stage C. At D we return to the public area of review and fine tuning in continued action.

Clearly, pedagogy which operates only at the public level denies the learner the opportunity to make sense and to accommodate new information into existing structures. An important element in that reconstruction process is the opportunity to reflect in and on practice. Equally important, given the frameworks supplied by Norman and Gal'Perin, is the importance of

Figure 9.2: A Vygotskian Cycle (after Harré, 1983)

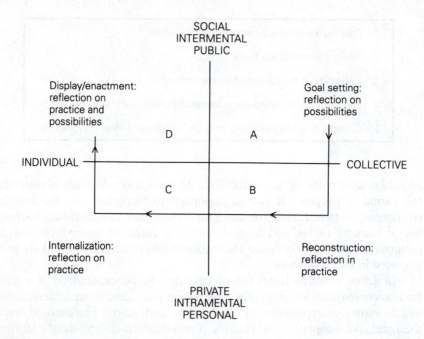

dialogue in all four quadrants and of the important pedagogical role to be managed by the mediator as the learner works through the quadrants and moves from interdependency to independence.

The use of action research cycles in adult learning is relatively common-place. Nevertheless, we need to examine the process in sufficient detail to inform our understanding of the role of the change-agent within it. If we compare a typical action research cycle with our adaptation of Harré's model we will recognize both similarities and implications for staff development and adult learning.

A similar shifting between public and private obtains within this cycle (Figure 9.3), as observing, considering possibilities and planning equates with the social and collective concerns in quadrant A (Figure 9.2). The move to individual action planning and reflection in action is at a personal level which draws upon the concerns of the collective found in quadrant B. Monitoring and reflection on practice (Yinger, 1986) will occur in quadrant C which is the personal and individual domain. Review and evaluation in the public quadrant of individual/social occurs when individuals publicly assert their own claims to knowledge based upon their reflection on evidence of their own action. To take these learning cycles one step further is to examine the shifting function of dialogue within the cycle and the importance of inter-action with the 'other' throughout the process and not only in the public domains of quadrants A and D. Reflection on practice has to be more than a solitary activity if learning is to occur.

Figure 9.3: An Action Research Spiral

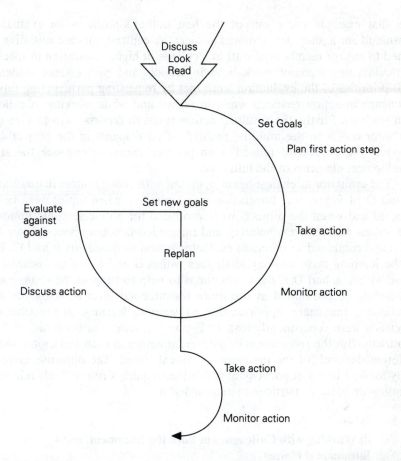

Discuss
Look
Read

Set Goals

Plan first action step

Set new goals

Evaluate
against
goals

Take action

Replan

Discuss action

Monitor action

Take action

Monitor action

The potential contribution of the mediator or mentor is evident in such an account of the learning cycle within the action research spiral. However, current strategies for the deployment of action research within whole-school and cross-curricular development projects, does complicate the conceptualization of such individual/collective and public/private learning processes. Indeed, the classic action-research mode of the individual/isolated practitioner undertaking unaided research in his or her own classroom might now be considered to be anachronistic. Instead, it is useful to examine some contemporary case-studies of the learning relationship within programmes of practitioner research and development.

Three examples may serve to illustrate the importance of talk at the private intramental level of the teacher learning process. The first is a college-based study which serves as a warning, the second is a school-based success and the third originates in a consultancy contract with an LEA curriculum development project.

i) Keeping to the Intermental Plane

The first example arose out of the first author's work as an evaluator-consultant on a staff development project. A centrally-funded initiative, it aimed to engage members of staff in a college of higher education in specific curriculum development work both in schools and with college students. Two priorities of the evaluation were met by requesting participating tutors to engage in action research while in school and while working in college with students. Firstly, the resulting action research reports were to give the evaluator access to the multiple realities of participants in the project and secondly the process of reflection on practice aimed to enhance the staff development elements of the initiative.

The evaluator as change-agent operated with college tutors in quadrants A and D of Figure 9.2. Interaction was limited to when topics were being selected and when the projects were produced for public scrutiny. Funding restrictions and an overwhelming and misguided concern about privacy for reflection combined to preclude evaluator access to quadrants B and C. But in the learning cycle analogy, dialogues within B and C are as essential as those within A and D if the evaluator is to help to support the change and not simply be positioned at the more instrumental level of instigator and scrutinizer. Important opportunities to support learning and encourage extension were consequently lost. In Figure 9.2, reflection occurs in all four quadrants. But the reflection is of a different nature in each and should make different demands of the mediator as critical friend. The differing, increasingly focused forms of participant reflection, require a responsively adaptive relationship between participant and mediator.

ii) Working with Colleagues at both the Intermental and Intramental Planes

We have already summarized the goal of the relationship as the move to independence through interdependence. Such a process is evident in the case of Jill, a reception class teacher and team leader, who took her three colleagues through an action research cycle in which all four teachers developed ways of enhancing pupil learning in the wet sand activity areas of their classrooms. Jill initiated discussion with her colleagues. Acting 'as if' her fellow teachers shared her concern for fine pedagogic details, she set up a review of practice, facilitated goal setting for children's behaviour and provided, at her colleagues' request, appropriate classroom stimuli. In this case workcards from the local teachers centre were selected by the participating teachers from a collection provided by Jill. Control shifted from Jill to her colleagues as they moved to the second stage of monitoring and mutual support. Through regular informal meetings and exchange of information amongst the group of teachers, reflection in practice was regularly enhanced by a continuously discussed process of reflection on practice by the group.

The analogy here with Norman's restructuring process (Norman, 1978) and Gal'Perin's stages 2 and 3 'taking practical action steps' and 'talking about the action and its implications' (after Gal'Perin, 1970) is clear. The teachers quickly came to own and internalize the change, publicly asserted their claims to it and independently pressed for a similar approach to another area of classroom work. Jill worked with them in quadrant A as she secured their adoption of the need for change by acting 'as if' her colleagues regularly focused on the fine detail of their pedagogy. She then set up contracts with them that ensured that they worked through quadrants B and C in supported privacy while they internalized their increased understanding of pedagogy. At the evaluation, review and plan stage they moved into quadrant D and confidently directed their own activities to another area of provision in their classrooms.

Jill succeeded in her twin aims of improving pedagogy in a specific area of the curriculum and in empowering her colleagues in the discourse of children's learning. This exercise was successful because Jill carefully managed the pedagogic tension, more evident perhaps in adult learning than elsewhere, of the need to maintain interdependence in order to allow eventual independence. The sharing of knowledge amongst the teachers both facilitated and was facilitated by increased competency in recognizing and discussing the abilities of four and five year olds. The teachers became participants in the discourse of children's learning and thinking through an interdependent dialogue within the private domain and finally independently demonstrated the use of that discourse in their claims for appropriate provision for the age group.

iii) Supporting Teachers as They Work Through the Cycle

The third example provides an alternative view of the ways in which practitioners may be initiated into the procedures of action research and development and encouraged to integrate these procedures into their on-going professional practice. This example comes from the second author's role as evaluation consultant to a curriculum project in a Local Education Authority. As part of this consultancy, the writer worked with another colleague to support a group of teachers from a number of different schools in fulfilling their roles as equal opportunities coordinators. A strategy adopted involved the consultants working in partnership with the coordinators to develop their reflective skills and to facilitate the organization of sustained intervention in equal opportunities issues.

The strategy may be related to the four quadrants outlined in Figure 9.2 as follows. Initially, the consultants worked as mediators with the coordinators by conducting detailed review sessions on an individual basis, both to inform the mediator's view of the complexity of the anticipated change-process, and to introduce the co-ordinators to the value of structured, mediated reflection on possible strategies for development. From this, the consultants developed a conceptual framework for thinking about equal opportunities and a developmental model for the potential organization of action. This model was presented to the coordinators during a series of INSET sessions, in order to help them explore the various value issues inherent within it, and to enable them to identify each school's current position *vis-à-vis* the model. The exploration was designed to enhance the coordinator's ability to undertake reflection-on-practice, to perceive deeper meanings and social dimensions inherent within their professional practices through discussion of a shared model.

The next stage of activity moved the group into the intramental plane, quadrants B and C (Figure 9.2) as the consultants acted as supervisors for the coordinators who undertook a programme of innovation in their own schools. The programme was devised by the coordinator but located within the frameworks for action research and development already described. The consultants provided supervision and support for these activities, both through individual counselling sessions and through collective review sessions. Both supervision strategies were designed to stimulate the coordinators' reflection on the experience of managing systematic innovation and enhance their ability to integrate reflection into their continuing professional practice.

At the end of the first development phase of the project, a summative review process was organized by the consultants to allow the coordinators to make explicit what had been achieved both in terms of the improved provision for equal opportunities within the schools and of their own professional development. At this stage, Harré's quadrant D, a new relationship between consultants and coordinators was negotiated, reflecting the increased competence of the practitioners in managing action research and processes evaluation and giving them a greater degree of autonomy in pursuit of their professional goals.

So far we have emphasized the importance of dialogue throughout the process of learning: from exploring possibilities, through discussing practice, to reviewing and displaying outcomes. The part to be played by self-evaluation within the reflective dialogue cycle also needs consideration. Self-evaluation in the infant school and LEA examples was certainly empowering and in tune with Taylor's views on agentic selfhood.

> But in at least our modern notion of self, responsibility has a stronger sense. We think of the agent not only as partly responsible for what he does, for the degree to which he acts in line with his evaluations, but also as responsible in some sense for those evaluations (Taylor, 1977, p. 118).

For Taylor, to take responsibility for self-evaluation is to take part in one's own identity construction. Self-evaluating teachers are therefore engaged in constructing a professional identity which is effective and purposeful. The view of learning which we recognize to be implicit within our model of the reflective practitioner (see Figure 9.2) calls into question any simplistic notion of self-evaluation as an action which is entirely private. Rather we would like to emphasize the function of the mediator or 'other', whether mentor, inservice tutor, curriculum co-ordinator or similar role, in the reflective practitioner process. We would therefore wish to remain mindful of Taylor's qualifying 'in some sense' the notion of responsibility for evaluation.

Those who support teacher reflection play an important part in moving the process from the public to the private domain before assisting a return to public assertion of claims to knowledge. But the mentor role is embedded in a complex wider context. In the initial moves from public to private, from intermental to intramental, from the social-collective to the collective-personal, they are operating in a set of processes which both aid the internalization of cultural emphases and, according to Ball (1990), employ self-regulation as a means of social control. Ball identifies a number of different ways in which the personal motives and characteristics of teachers (and pupils) are made subject to public scrutiny and organizational regulation. Teacher appraisal, for example, may encourage personal reflection and self-disclosure in ways that facilitate new modes of managerial surveillance and institutional control. Rose (1990), meanwhile, argues that this process is central to modern citizenship and that the development of new technologies of social control based upon humanistic and social psychology potentially transforms the possibilities of personal autonomy and collective existence. It is consequently important that individuals who fulfil mediator roles in processes of professional reflection, self-evaluation and action research are conscious of these political dimensions of their work, and operate within ethical guidelines and organizational procedures which make explicit what is at stake in terms of professional autonomy and organizational regulation.

Clearly, from Taylor's perspective self-evaluation enhances a sense of purposeful control over events and is hence motivating and from Rose's it has a regulatory function which has as its rationale the well-being of the community. Neither analyst justifies self-evaluation as the route to effective learning. Tharp and Gallimore (1991), as we have already seen, take us further with their view of performance-enhancing regulation which includes the mediator or 'other'. This once more returns us to the quality of the relationship between the reflective practitioner and 'other', and to earlier discussions on the place of dialogue in teaching and learning.

We would wish to argue that dialogue is as central to the cycle of reflection on practice as it is to the view of learning we have been proposing (see e.g. Figure 9.1). Elements of the action research movement have emphasized the importance of space to talk, and empowerment through giving practitioners their voices (Miller, 1990), but many have largely focused on the critical friend relationship in evaluation and harked back to Habermas (1970) and notions of symmetry of control in ideal speech situations (Carr and Kemmis, 1986). We suggest that a greater complexity obtains. We believe that a symmetry does exist, but that it is carefully managed by the mediator in order to first induct and then to engage the teacher/learner as an effective participant within a professional discourse.

We have noted that the balance of power within the dialogue shifts as the learner/action researcher moves through the cycle outlined in Figure 9.2. Jill, in the infant school example discussed earlier, started by inducting her colleagues into the discourse by acting 'as if' they were already participants in the discourse. She controlled the discourse but started a process of their acquisition of it. Edwards (1988) discusses 'as if' behaviour as a strategy frequently used by infant teachers as they induct children into a variety of discourses. As the teachers reviewed, monitored and discussed their own actions they became more equal partners in the conversation until, as they moved into the final stage of evaluation, review and plan, they were able to take control of the dialogue and direct future actions. Jill managed the conversations at each stage of the process to enable her colleagues to gain access to and eventually flexible use of the discourse of pedagogy.

We are familiar with the current orthodoxies in educational consultancy concerning power-equalization in the consultant-client relationship and the need for neutral and non-directive intervention strategies by consultants (Gray, 1988; Aubrey, 1990). We would suggest, however, that there is a need for further research into the ways in which mediator/practitioner roles are conducted in practice and for further analysis of the complexities of such professional relationships. These proposals signal our commitment to the potential value of the mediator's role in facilitating professional reflection and self-evaluation.

We also propose that appropriate management of dialogue enables mediators to support practitioners through coping with change and the identity shifts that result from the learning process. Our notion of supported reflection on practice has as its aim the independent functioning of the practitioner and suggests that the mediator role may be analogous to that of the counsellor. The comparison of critical friend or consultant with counsellor is not new, (Murgatroyd, 1988), but it may help us to consider the relationship between learning and reflection on practice.

Teacher learning all too frequently involves monitoring and engaging with processes of identity threatening change. Consequently the role of mediator or 'other' may merge with that of counsellor as supporter of individuals or groups. Murgatroyd (1988), talking of the evaluator-consultant, indicates four dispositions necessary to the role: accurate empathy, positive regard, genuineness and concreteness. All four may be equally applied to any mediator involved in supporting teacher reflection.

Within this context, reflection in teacher learning may acquire an additional meaning as teachers' concerns are reflected back in counselling-style dialogues designed to empower the practitioners to take control of their own learning and development. The emergence of the articulate, informed and confident practitioner should be an outcome of the mediator as counsellor role. But this demands that further attention is paid not simply to the appropriate disposition in counselling/mediator roles. The mediator's role in terms of the structuring and re-structuring of both the learning process and the professional relationship requires further consideration. The management and identification of the discrete phases of professional growth in supervisory settings is central to the development of increasingly autonomous reflective practitioners.

Our model of reflection supported by carefully managed dialogues also has broader implications for practice both in higher education and in school-based staff development. While peer networks are important, there is, we suggest, a vital role to be played by the mediator in assisting adult learning. If teacher self-evaluation is to subsume a notion of teacher learning then the importance of reflection and the support it requires should be warranted by appropriate staffing, training and resourcing. There is a danger that the very ubiquity of the 'reflective practitioner' may in fact produce a degradation of meaning. It is our concern to ensure that professional development means more than self-regulation, but takes teacher learning as a central concern both within the initial training of teachers and within their continuing INSET provision.

References

AUBREY, C. (ed.) (1990) *Consultancy in the United Kingdom*, Lewes: Falmer.

BALL, S.J. (1990) 'Management as Moral Technology: A Luddite Analysis', in BALL, S.J. (ed.) *Foucault and Education: Disciplines and Knowledge*, London: Routledge.

BENNETT, S.N., DESFORGES, C., COCKBURN, A. and WILKINSON, B. (1984) *The Quality of Pupil Learning Experiences*, London: Lawrence Erlbaum Associates.

CARR, W. and KEMMIS, S. (1986) *Becoming Critical*, Lewes: Falmer.

DAY, C. (1985) 'Professional Learning and Researcher Intervention: an action research perspective', *British Educational Research Journal*, **11**(2), pp. 133–51.

DES (1990) *Developing School Management: The Way Forward*, London: HMSO.

ELLIOT, J. (1991) *Action Research for Educational Change*, Milton Keynes: Open University Press.

EDWARDS, A. (1988) 'Power Games in Early Education', *Early Child Development and Care*, **34**, pp. 143–9.

GAL'PERIN, P. (1970) 'An experimental study in the formation of mental actions', in STONES, E. (ed.) *Readings in Educational Psychology*, London: Methuen.

GRAY, H.L. (ed.) (1988) *Management Consultancy in Schools*, London: Cassell.

HABERMAS, J. (1970) 'Towards a Theory of Communicative Competence', in DREITZEL, H.P. (ed.) *Recent Sociology*, **2**., New York: Macmillan.

HARRE, R. (1983) *Personal Being*, Oxford: Blackwell.

HOPKINS, D. (1985) *A Teacher's Guide to Action Research*, Milton Keynes: Open University Press.

LIGHT, P. and PERRET-CLERMONT, A.N. (1991) 'Social Context Effects in Learning and Testing', in LIGHT, P. *et al.* (eds) *Learning to Think*, London: Routledge.

MILLER, J.L. (1990) *Creating Spaces and Finding Voices*, New York: State University of New York Press.

MURGATROYD, S. (1988) 'Consulting and Counselling: The Theory and Practice of Structural Counselling', in GRAY, H.L. (ed.) *Management Consultancy in Schools*, London: Cassell.

NORMAN, D.A. (1978) 'Notes towards a complex theory of learning', in LESGOLD, A.M. *et al.* (eds) *Cognitive Psychology and Instruction*, New York: Plenum.

ROSE, N. (1990) 'Psychology as a Social Science', in PARKER, I. and SHOTTER, J. (eds) *Deconstructing Social Psychology*, London: Routledge and Kegan Paul.

SMYTH, W.J. (1988) 'An alternative and critical perspective for clinical supervision in schools', in SMYTH, J. (ed.) *A Critical Pedagogy of Teacher Evaluation*, Geelong: Deakin Unviersity Press.

TAYLOR, C. (1977) 'What is Human Agency?' in MISCHEL, T. (ed.) *The Self*, Oxford: Blackwell.

THARP, R. and GALLIMORE, R. (1991) 'A Theory of Teaching as Assisted Performance', in LIGHT, P. *et al.* (eds) *Learning to Think*, London: Routledge.

VYGOTSKY, L.S. (1978) *Mind in Society*, Cambridge: Harvard University Press.

— (1991) 'Genesis of the Higher Mental Functions' in LIGHT, P. *et al.* (eds) *Learning to Think*, London: Routledge.

WALKERDINE, V. (1988) *The Mastery of Reason*, London: Routledge.

WERTSCH, J.R. (1985) *Culture, Communication and Cognition*, Cambridge: Cambridge University Press.

YINGER, R.J. (1986) 'Examining Thought in-Action: A Theoretical and Methodolgoical Critique of Research on Interactive Teaching', *Teaching and Teacher Education*, **2**(3), pp. 263–82.

Notes on Contributors

David Brunton is Senior Lecturer at St Martin's College, Lancaster, England.

James Calderhead is Professor of Education at the University of Bath, England.

Anne Edwards is Director of Research at St Martin's College, Lancaster, England.

Peter Gates is Lecturer in Mathematics Education at the University of Bath, England.

J. Gary Knowles is Assistant Professor of Education at the University of Michigan, USA.

Vicki Kubler LaBoskey is Assistant Professor of Education at Mills College, California, USA.

G. Williamson McDiarmid is Co-Director of the National Center for Research on Teacher Learning at Michigan State University, USA.

Donald McIntyre is Reader in Education at Oxford University, England.

K. Anne Proctor is Senior Lecturer at Edge Hill College of Higher Education, Ormskirk, England.

Tom Russell is Professor of Education at Queen's University, Ontario, Canada.

Sarah Tann is Senior Lecturer at Oxford Polytechnic, England.

Linda Valli is Associate Professor and Director of Teacher Education at the Catholic University of America, Washington, USA.

Name Index

AACTE 40
AERA 46
Alexander, R.J. 40–1
Allport, G. 77
Andrew, M. 15
Anning, A. 58
Apple, M. 80
Applegate, J. 14
Arends, R. 14, 16
Arkoff, R. 54
Armstrong, J.R. 138
Ashton, P.M.E. 94
Aspinwal, K. 71, 83, 86
Aubrey, C. 164

Bain, L. 14, 16
Ball, D.L. 114, 118–19
Ball, S.J. 70, 162
Baptiste, H.P. 14, 16
Barnes, H. 12
Becker, H. 70, 72, 77
Benbow, C.P. 138
Bennett, S.N. 155
Berlak, A. 14, 17
Berlak, H. 14, 17
Berliner, D.C. 20, 56
Bertaux, D. 70
Bey, T.M. 81
Beynon, J. 70, 72–3
Biermann, M.J. 84
Bogdan, R. 72
Bolin, F.S. 80
Borko, H. 14, 16

Boud, D. 31, 58–9, 64
Boyd, E. 83–5
Boydell, D. 95
Brennan, M. 15, 83–6
Brophy, J.E. 135
Brown, S. 94
Bruner, J. 67
Brunton, D. 8
Buchmann, M. 32, 82–3
Bullough, R.V. 81
Butt, R. 84

Cairns, L.G. 94
Calderhead, J. 3, 4, 20, 23, 27, 42, 56, 145
Canning, C. 83–6
Carr, W. 1, 44, 54, 155–6, 163
Carter, K. 60
Charvoz, A. 84
Ciriello, M. 14
Clandinin, D.J. 83
Clark, C.M. 84
Clift, R. 13–6, 19–20
Cockburn, A. 155
Cogan, M.L. 94
Colbert, J.A. 81
Cole, A.L. 71
Connelly, F.M. 83
Cooper, J.E. 84
Corcoran, E. 15
Crow, N.A. 84

D.E.S. 154
Dawson, C.J. 109

168

Subject Index

action research, 2, 6, 8, 46, 155, 159
Alert Novices, 24–36
Alternate Route Programs, 117, 120, 152
apprenticeship of observation, 71
Approaches to Supervision, 109
ATTEP. 14, 17, 20

children's learning, 8, 113, 122, 130
clinical supervision, 94, 109
coaching, 2
common-sense Thinkers, 24–36
craft knowledge, 40, 48
critical theory, 1, 45, 54, 155

discipline, 14, 60, 63

experiential learning, 1, 8, 57, 149
expert novice differences, 43

gender beliefs, 119

intuition, 19, 33–4
Inservice programs, 120, 154, 162

knowledge base for teaching, 40

lesson planning, 60
levels of reflectivity, 12, 26, 35, 44–6, 84
Life histories, 70–88

Multiple Perspectives program, 15

New Hampshire program, 15

open-mindedness, 1, 26, 30
orientations to reflection, 4, 12–3, 43
oxford Internship program, 42, 46

pedagogical thinkers, 24–36
personal theories, 7, 55, 68
Practical deliberation, 35
Preconceptions of reflection, 31
Preconceptions of teaching, 55, 70
PROTEACH, 20, 116

reflection-in-action, 1, 83, 144
reflective journals, 2, 53, 73, 80
Reflective Teacher Education Programs,
    11
researcher as change agent, 160, 164
RITE, 14, 20

self-realization, 86
Staff Development, 117, 154, 165
STEP, 23
Stereotypes, 132, 139
supervising teaching, 45, 94

technical rationality, 12, 15–6, 44, 54
theory-practice relationship, 18, 39–40,
    47–51
Tutors' Judgments about Teaching, 45,
    99